F

Nineteenth-century Crime
PREVENTION AND PUNISHMENT

DAVID & CHARLES SOURCES FOR SOCIAL & ECONOMIC HISTORY

GENERAL EDITOR: *E. R. R. Green*
Director of the Institute of Irish Studies
The Queen's University of Belfast

FREE TRADE
Norman McCord
Reader in Modern History
University of Newcastle upon Tyne

THE FACTORY SYSTEM   VOLUME I BIRTH AND GROWTH
VOLUME II THE FACTORY SYSTEM
AND SOCIETY
J. T. Ward
Senior Lecturer in Economic History
University of Strathclyde

THE ENGLISH POOR LAW 1780–1930
Michael E. Rose
Lecturer in History, University of Manchester

READINGS IN THE DEVELOPMENT OF ECONOMIC ANALYSIS
R. D. Collison Black
Professor of Economics
The Queen's University of Belfast

EDUCATION: ELEMENTARY EDUCATION 1780–1900
J. M. Goldstrom
Lecturer in Economic and Social History
The Queen's University of Belfast

in preparation
ELECTIONEERING BEFORE 1832
Peter Jupp
Lecturer in Modern History, The Queen's University of Belfast

DAVID & CHARLES SOURCES FOR SOCIAL & ECONOMIC HISTORY

J. J. TOBIAS

Director of General Studies, The Police College,
Bramshill

Nineteenth-century Crime

PREVENTION AND PUNISHMENT

DAVID & CHARLES : NEWTON ABBOT

ISBN 0 7153 5709 3

Set in Baskerville 11 pt 2 pt leaded
and printed in Great Britain
by Latimer Trend & Company Limited Plymouth
for David & Charles (Publishers) Limited
South Devon House   Newton Abbot   Devon

Contents

Introduction

This book presents documents on the crime and criminals of the nineteenth century, and on society's response—its attempts to understand why people committed crimes, to prevent or detect their activities, and to punish them when it caught them. The subject is thus a large one, and the endeavour to represent all its aspects is made more difficult by the very great changes that occurred in the period under review. As in so many fields, the nineteenth century saw profound transformations of the criminal scene and of policing and prison methods, and much anxious discussion of these topics.

The opening section presents a selection of contemporary writings on the causation of crime. Crime was as popular a subject in the nineteenth century as it is today, and there were many who tried to explain its causes. The Royal Commission on a Constabulary Force of 1839—that is to say, Edwin Chadwick—destroyed the belief in a crude association between poverty and crime: 'The notion that any considerable proportion of the crimes against property are caused by blameless poverty or destitution we find disproved at every step.'* After publication of its seminal *Report*, few people saw the main cause of crime in a simple mechanistic model of hungry men driven to steal for lack of other means of gaining their bread. Nor were the Victorians foolish enough to ascribe criminal conduct entirely or mainly to 'evil natures.' The writers of the mid-nineteenth cen-

* Royal Commission on Constabulary Force, *PP* (1839), xix, 73 (para 65).

tury could see the many complex ways in which poverty of life and surroundings could often result in someone, especially a youngster, entering the ranks of the criminals. When the Rev W. D. Morrison in the 1890s presented what can be claimed to be the earliest scientific and methodical works on criminology written in the United Kingdom, he was consolidating the views of his day, and was not alone in insisting on the social rather than the personal causes of crime. By this time the poverty of social provision in British cities had been highlighted by *The Bitter Cry of Outcast London*, a savage attack on slum conditions published in 1883, and in the ensuing debate about housing the poor the connection with crime was not ignored.

This connection was the more important because criminals, like folk following many other trades, tended to congregate in particular districts. In St Giles's and around St George's, Southwark, and in other parts of London, there were mazes of narrow streets and courts where pursuit of a criminal might well be dangerous and would almost certainly be futile. Descriptions of these areas and their inhabitants abound, in newspapers, journals and descriptive or polemical books. The Victorian novelists, too, are witnesses whose voices should be heard. These writers, nearly all from the middle or upper classes, have indeed a tendency to write *de haut en bas*—as if criminals were creatures of a different species—but in view of the differences in life-styles this is almost forgivable, and it does not diminish the value of the evidence laid before us.

Some writers on crime and criminals in the nineteenth century tried to use in their work a quantitative approach which can only be applauded today. However, quantification in matters criminal is not easy, though much has been written on the subject in the past and in the present. In the nineteenth century many were prepared to regard the criminal statistics as a worthwhile source of evidence, and to submit them to detailed analysis. There were others who echoed the doubts of those modern thinkers who refer to 'the dark figure of crime' and regard the criminal returns as merely mapping the changing boundary between the seen and the unseen parts of the iceberg. Both sides in the debate are represented in the extracts that follow.

Discussion of the causation, nature and extent of crime obviously often led to a discussion of prevention. There was in the first part of the century a vigorous debate on methods of policing. As in every age, there was a price that society was not prepared to pay for the reduction of the level of crime, and at first the belief that an efficient police force was a threat to liberty prevented a thorough-going reform of the ancient machinery of law enforcement. Robert Peel showed, by the creation of the Metropolitan Police in 1829, that a police force could operate against criminals without instituting the tyranny of a police state, and thereafter the debate turned from the fundamental question of the existence of an efficient police—discussed, *inter alia*, by select committees of the House of Commons in 1816–18, 1822 and 1828—to matters of machinery, such as the organisation of the police and its relationship to national and local government—discussed by a Royal Commission in 1839 and a select committee in 1853. In the administrative revolution of the nineteenth century the old systems of policing were swept away and replaced by an orderly bureaucratic organisation.

In much the same way, and with just as much argument, the prison system was overhauled. There was a difference, however: while the 1829 solution to the problem of policing was accepted with little challenge for many years thereafter, no such unanimity prevailed on the question of punishment. By the accession of Queen Victoria there was, it is true, virtual agreement on the use of capital punishment, which was more or less reserved for murder; corporal punishment, though discussed from time to time by those concerned with the problems of reforming youngsters, was not a major subject of controversy. But there was much discussion about the main method of punishment, which was imprisonment. The treatment of convicts transported overseas, the system of transportation itself,

and the handling of criminals confined in prisons in this country
—always the majority of those sentenced by the courts to imprisonment of any kind—all these topics were furiously debated.
The unreformed prisons of the sort that John Howard had seen
found few advocates, but there were a number of different
attempts to apply the rationality of the nineteenth century to
the problem of imprisonment. If the systems devised in the
name of rationality seem to us to have failed to consider the
demands of humanity, this should not lead us into a wholesale
condemnation of those who sought constructive solutions to a
problem that is still unsolved today.

In all our modern discussions of the crime and criminals of
the nineteenth century, there is one voice that cannot be
directly heard—the criminals themselves cannot speak to us. It
is true that there are books written by educated people who
found themselves in prison, and we have statements supposed to
have been taken from prisoners themselves and written down as
if in their own words (examples of both sorts will be found in
this book). Yet educated criminals were atypical, and a
prisoner talking to a journalist, prison chaplain, investigator or
any other representative of the middle classes may perhaps not
always have spoken his mind, and in any event his words come
to us at secondhand. It is possible for someone who has soaked
himself in the literature of the period to feel that he understands
the ideas and aspirations of Victorian policemen, magistrates or
workers for penal reform. It is possible for him to feel that he
can picture the criminal scene as it was perceived by such
people. But he can never see through the eyes of the criminals
themselves. He has to be content with what he can learn from
those many earnest people who grappled so desperately, and on
the whole with such humanity, with the overwhelming problem of the causation and nature of crime.

Contemporary Views
on the Causation of Crime

The spirit of scientific inquiry which was one aspect of nineteenth-century thought led to much study of the causation of crime, and many of these early writings are surprisingly modern in tone. Victorians with knowledge of the subject did not all regard crime as a product of the evil nature of the criminals. There was indeed a belief in a 'criminal class' (see Part Two), but much of the discussion on the forces that led people (especially the young) into crime was sympathetic and understanding. John Clay, Chaplain of Preston House of Correction (33), said of the youngsters who came into his prison, 'I do not suppose they have ever heard a dozen kind words spoken to them at their homes'; William Crauford, 'Gratuitous Secretary of the Society to Inquire into the Causes of Juvenile Delinquency', told a Select Committee of the House of Commons in 1817, 'It is very easy to blame these poor children, and to ascribe their misconduct to an innate propensity to vice; but I much question whether any human being, circumstanced as many of them are, can reasonably be expected to act otherwise'.

Nineteenth-century opinion often tended, indeed, to seek causes for crime in general—like searching for the causes of 'disease'—but looked in what seem to us to be the right places. The Victorians directed their attention to social problems, especially those of the large towns, which shaped the destiny of the poor and drove many of them to seek in criminal acts solu-

11

tions to their difficulties. Drink was of course often put forward
as a cause of crime. Sometimes the point was made in loose
terms—the beer which used to be a beverage accompanying
food was now, wrote William Hoyle in 1876, 'mainly used as
part of a habit of tippling, which fills the land with drunkenness, crime, pauperism, insanity, and a host of other festering
evils'. Other writers spoke more moderately of the connection
between drink and crime (1). The other causes of crime suggested in the extracts in this part accord well enough with
modern thinking. Indeed, it will be seen that the arguments of
the present-day interactionist school, which sees a criminal
career as being often an acceptance by an individual of the role
society has thrust upon him, are foreshadowed in the work of
W. D. Morrison (4) and in the case-history recounted by
Benjamin Waugh (3).

1 Rev J. W. Horsley   Drink and Crime

The Rev J. W. Horsley (1845–1921) was Chaplain at
Clerkenwell Prison from 1876 to 1886, and then Secretary of
the Waifs and Strays Society. From 1889 until his retirement
in 1911 he held livings in the poorer parts of London, and
was active in local government, becoming Mayor of Southwark in 1910. He wrote a number of books about his experiences, from which one gains the impression that he was
shrewd, energetic and humane. He had the crypt of his
church at Walworth cleared of coffins and turned into a
playground for poor children, and as a member of the Woolwich Board of Guardians he drew attention to the mono-
tonous uniforms of the girls in the Banstead Poor Law
Schools: 'When dress-stuff for 600 girls has to be bought, why
need it be all of one colour?' He observed the petty criminals
of London (or at any rate the unsuccessful ones) at close
quarters, and his testimony as to the part drink played in
their life may be accepted as accurate, though it should be
noted that he was a member of the council of the Church of
England Temperance Society.

Let none imagine that no prisons or police-courts would be needed but for the facilities for and the habits of drinking; but yet in the absence of the liquor traffic one police-court and one prison would certain be sufficient for the Metropolis. Thus one day I obtained a return from Marylebone Police Court and found—

Monday,	59 charges, of which 49 for drunkenness.
Tuesday,	29 ,, ,, 20 ,, ,,
Wednesday,	23 ,, ,, 22 ,, ,,
Thursday,	9 ,, ,, 7 ,, ,,
Friday,	23 ,, ,, 15 ,, ,,
Saturday,	11 ,, ,, 11 ,, ,,
	154 124

Sometimes those who are concerned to minimise the evils and the national expense caused by drinking, quote the numbers given in official statistics as being charged with drunkenness or as being drunk and disorderly, and assuming that this is all show what a small portion they bear to the general population, or even to the total of offences of all descriptions. Thus under the head of non-indictable offences in the last year for which we have the Judicial Statistics the grand total of persons apprehended or dealt with on summons is 628,265, of whom only 169,344 are under the head of Drunkenness. Even this means that more than a quarter of the offenders were drunk, but no one who had gone into the cases of the rest, or even read a daily paper, would be ignorant of the fact that by a most moderate estimate half the cases of common assaults, three-quarters of assaults on the police, and half the aggravated assaults, were committed by drunken persons. This would give us 28,294—8,592—953, total 37,839, to add to the 169,344 bringing it up to 207,183. Cruelty to animals and cruelty to children again account together for 15,660 cases, and of these half might fairly be considered directly drink-caused, as also might be half of the 10,773 cases of malicious damage of the ordinary kind, window smashing and so forth, and half of such military and naval offences (chiefly desertion), as come before the police-courts to the number of 4,560. These moieties would come to 15,496, and would bring the drink charges up to 222,679. Then one knows the number of cases under other heads, under nearly every head, in fact, which are indirectly caused by drink, *e.g.*, thefts by or from drunken persons, and one speedily arrives at the conclusion that to estimate half all crime as directly, and an additional one-fourth as indirectly, drink-caused, is a moderate estimate and below that which most experts, such as judges, magistrates, chief constables, and prison officials, have over and over again given as the result of their observation. Then further, one has to note that the police figures only account for such drunkards and for such drink-caused offences as have come under the cognisance of the law, and by no means give the full amount of the national expense, or loss, or nuisance for which intemperance is responsible. Any doctor, parish priest, or relieving officer would know that of every ten persons known to him as frequently or even habitually intemperate not more than one or two had come into the hands of the police. The police figures give, in fact, only one item, and that by no means the largest, in the bill the nation has to present against intemperance as a cause of unnecessary and easily preventible expenditure or loss.

Further to emphasise the point that the minimisers of the evil and national loss caused by drink are but misleading people when they attempt to confine the effects of intemperance as a cause of crime to those cases in which the word 'drink' appears on the charge-sheet or in the calendar, I take the following cases from a page of my note-book. Not one of them suggests drunkenness in the title of the offence, and yet in every one drink was the chief and generally the sole cause of the crime.

Stealing pony and cart.—A young man out on his employer's business spends some of the money he had collected in a public-house, and therefore fears to face his master, and recollecting the devil's proverb, 'As well be hung for a sheep as a lamb,' sells the pony and cart. As he expressed the matter to me, 'The first word of your mouth when you're drunk is you don't care for nothing—so there you are!'

Desertion.—A young soldier, aged 21. He had five times been fined in the army for being drunk, got drunk again, knew he would be court-martialled, and so deserted, having made away with his kit to get drink as his pay had been stopped for the fine.

Uttering.—A man, aged 35, charged with passing bad money, to which mean form of theft, which especially injures the poorer trades-people, he had descended. He was once a master-baker, then a tobacconist, and went down and down till he got to be a mere fourpenny lodging-house man. He had been separated from his wife through his drunkenness, had five brothers, four of whom had died through drink, all six of the family having been heavy drinkers.

Criminal assault on his stepdaughter, aged thirteen, on a Saturday night, after he had been drinking from ten to twelve with his mates, and then with his wife all the day up to 9 p.m.

Larceny.—A married woman, aged 35, stole thirty shillings from her landlady to get drink; spent it all in liquor. 'My husband coaxes me, and does everything he can to help me from drink—including beating.'

Larceny.—A woman, aged 52, stole from the publican whose servant she had been for three months. Twenty-seven empty spirit bottles found in her room.

Arson.—An ancient of 73 years, locked up for being drunk, set fire to his cell.

Indecency.—The man had four previous convictions (of three, three, twelve, and six months) for the same offence, which was only thought of and committed when drunk.

Illegal pawning.—A married woman, with three children left out of seven, stole various articles from her landlady so that she might get drink money without her husband's knowledge.

Begging.—A woman, aged 44, seven out of ten children alive, her husband fairly well to do, begged simply to get money for drink.

Burglary.—A married woman, had been intemperate for four years. Frequent rows therefore with her husband. Afraid to go home because she had been drinking in the afternoon; therefore she stayed out, and at half-past three broke into a public-house to get more drink.

Theft.—A medical man, aged 43, had once his carriage and pair and published several books. Lost all through drinking though he had been a teetotaler up to the age of 33. J. W. Horsley. *Prisons and Prisoners* (1898), 86–91.

---

2 Rev H. Worsley   The Causes of Rural Crime

The causation of crime was a favourite subject for a favourite Victorian exercise, the prize essay. The Rev Henry Worsley, a recently ordained country vicar, published in 1849 his book *Juvenile Depravity*, which had won him a prize of £100 offered by an anonymous donor. The advertisement announcing the competition had said: 'The fearful and growing prevalence of Juvenile Depravity, and the inadequacy of the various means hitherto employed to meet the evil, have long challenged inquiry. . . . No one . . . can fail to corroborate the testimony of the highest authorities in the land, that the monster evil of our country, and the source, directly or indirectly, of the greater portion of Juvenile Depravity and Crime is Intemperance'. Given this firm lead, Worsley did indeed place particular emphasis on the evils of drink; like others of the genre, his book is primarily a collection of the conventional thinking of the day (which of course increases its value for us). However, his comments on rural crime may perhaps have something of personal observation behind them.

The sources of crime in rural districts are chiefly the four following: beer-shops, the game laws, the tramp system, and the arrangements of cottages and lodging-houses.

Beer-shops very frequently do not exist in those villages which are under the immediate eye of some presiding tutelary guardian, or in other words, of a resident gentleman landowner: but wherever such influence is removed, they have sprung up with astonishing rapidity and in dense numbers. It is impossible to consider their effects on our rural population, except in connexion with the demoralizing habit of poaching. Intemperance and poaching act and re-act, the one vile habit on the other. "Poaching", says a witness examined by the late Select Committee of the Game Laws, "induces men and boys to be out at night, and brings them into connexion with individuals of very bad character, and carries them into those abominably bad places, the beer-shops. No crimes are so much on the increase as those against the game laws, or are so much affecting the condition of the rural population." It is in the beer-shops that individuals of notorious character meet, it is here they concoct their plans, and carouse before putting them in execution; the beer retailer is very frequently associated with the poachers, and to him they dispose of their plunder in payment for liquor. Poachers are glad to enlist boys in their service, whom they think they can trust, and they lead on these juvenile delinquents by insinuating the hope that, even should they be detected, their youth will screen them from punishment. Thus early introduction to the beer-shop, connexion with profligate companions, and habituation to one crime, poaching, demoralize and totally deprave a large portion of the youth among our rural poor. To steal game is not regarded as a sin among the villagers; and thus the precipice of crime is sloped to an inclined plane. From poaching the youthful delinquent proceeds to petty larceny, from this to some greater offence; the distinction in the mind between right and wrong once confused, to which the lax notion common to the poor on the subject of poaching very much tends, there is nothing to oppose the onward progress of crime until it issues in some most atrocious act. In proof of what I have advanced, the following is striking, written at the dictation of a poacher, and extracted from Prison Reports, 1846:

"When I first began poaching I lived with my father, and we had a dog that was much given to catching game. One time a man saw him kill a hare; this man kept a beer-shop; he said he would pay me well if I would let him have it. I was to go to his home at night. He gave me a glass of rum and 1s. 6d., and he wanted me to bring him another hare; I stopped drinking until I had spent the money. He told me I should get some snares, and he brought me some to look at, and showed me how to set them. I caught a hare that night, and took it to him, and I had it all in drink but 8d., and that I bought some wire with to make snares; and then I got to going to his house constantly, and taking hares there, and drinking ale and spirits of all kinds; and I think that beer-shop was the ruin of me."

One witness examined by the Committee on the Game Laws, 1845, says—"One case I knew of a man living on the borders of Worcestershire. He brought up four youths, his sons, to poaching; they went on from bad to worse, till now only one son remains in this country."

In evidence of the notion which the poor entertain on the subject of poaching, I cite the following:—"J. K., age 24, labourer, single. Three months, poaching. Been three times before for similar offences. *There is a difference between poaching and stealing. I should not steal myself.* Was never at school; all that I have learnt has been in prison. I had no work; they would not employ me because I had been a poacher. . . . I was caught with a leveret. I do not think I might have taken any thing else; *the leveret is wild. Many people would be friends with a poacher, but would not like to be very great friends with a man convicted of felony*."

Another witness before the Select Committee states:— "When I was about twenty-two, I became possessed of very large farms in Wiltshire, to the amount of between 2000 and 3000 acres, and I detected a poacher, a man who was wiring hares. He was proceeded against, and committed to gaol for three months. He was bringing up a large family as a labourer, and without any assistance from the parish, and, I believe, was only an occasional poacher. But as soon as he left the gaol at the end of three months, he became a *regular poacher, and an inhabitant of the public-house.*"

The noted Beer-shop Act of 1830, is, doubtless, one of the main causes of the increase of poaching; but the fact, that at the present day there is the antagonism of class against class in our rural districts, the association in country sports no longer subsisting as it did once, many of the sportsmen visiting their seats only in the shooting season, and remaining there no longer than this continues, or only for a few weeks at its commencement, is a powerful auxiliary cause.

The ill effects, however, of beer-shops in the rural districts, extend beyond those connected with the breach of the game laws. One witness examined by the Parliamentary Commission, states, that three-fourths of the rural crime is caused by them; and that the youngest boys, as well as evil-disposed persons, assemble there, and imbibe the rudiments of wickedness of all kinds. . . .

The great increase of late years in poaching, is a striking feature in rural crime. In the three years from 1827 to 1830, no fewer than 8,502 persons were convicted under the game laws. The increase since that period has been startling. In 1843, the committals for this offence amounted to 4,529. In 1844–45, and up to May 1846, that is during a period of 18 months, the convictions were 11,372, which gives an average of 4,834 per annum. . . .

All that is connected with poaching, tends to give to the habitual offender under this head, a tone of character at once daring and brutal. And it is to the great increase of this crime, and the associate ill effects of the beer-shop, that we with justice ascribe the many acts of sanguinary violence, the horrid tragedies of atrocious murder, which have defiled within very recent memory many scenes of rural life, and tainted spots, which have often been supposed, but very falsely at the present day, to be the favoured recesses of comfort, peace, and virtue.
H. Worsley. *Juvenile Depravity* (1849), 63–72

3 B. Waugh   A Case-history

Benjamin Waugh (1839–1908), a Congregational minister, was a member of the London School Board from 1870 to 1876, an active promoter of legislation to protect children, and a leading member of the group that founded the National Society for the Prevention of Cruelty to Children. He established a 'Wastepaper and Blacking Brigade' to care for vagrant boys, and local magistrates would hand first offenders over to this body instead of imprisoning them. His *The Gaol Cradle: Who Rocks It?*, published in 1876, is a powerful plea for the abolition of imprisonment of juveniles. It includes this case-history on the effects of the lack of social provision in the towns.

Fairly consider the following events, which we know of our own knowledge, and which we see no reason to regard as other than a fair tableaux of the ordinary course of things, and ask, Towards what does youthful imprisonment tend?

Let us premise that the incidents which follow are not recorded to reflect upon the administrators of the law, however they may excite the sympathy of the reader, and perhaps fill him with shame that as a citizen he is a party to such procedure. It is with the law, and not in any degree whatsoever with the officers of the law, rests the responsibility they imply. They are intended to show the *natural tendency* of imprisonment, alike for the erring lad and for, as I conceive, the erring State.

*   *   *   *   *   *

"The mother's dead; the boy has gone to gaol!" Thus spoke a Relieving Officer to a Board of Guardians in explanation of 4s. 8d. which was not now needed for out-door relief.

"Mother dead." She had been dying eleven months, and should have been bedridden all that time, but had dragged about till within the last few weeks. For twelve years after her faithless husband abandoned her, she took in washing. Those years had been a long, weary struggle against ill-health. Finally, cancer conquered the honest creature, and laid her on a pauper's bed. At two o'clock in the morning, alone, on the sacking-bottom of a four-post bed, she died!

Three days before she died, her only child—a boy—went out to beg. Cancer has a mighty hunger. To its wants, parish allowance was insufficient. The boy did not take kindly to begging, was naturally proud; but he loved his mother, and love conquered. The narrow, filthy street had in it scarcely a noisier or kindlier soul. He set out on his expedition. In two days—eleven miles away from home, unwashed and hungry-looking, he stood before a magistrate, charged with begging and having five shillings in his pocket! He was committed for three months with hard labour, the magistrate observing, "We *must* put a stop to this sort of thing."

*   *   *   *   *   *

It is getting dark. The latch of the door of a second-floor room—where sit a man, his wife, and two children round a table with a candle and tea-things on it—is quietly lifted.

"Who's there?" said a kindly voice.

"I was looking for my mother," timidly replied the intruder.

"Your mother! I know what you want, you gaol-bird! Out! you skulking thief!"

The kindly tone had changed to thunder. The shorn head, the pale face, stamped the inquirer a villain, and the voice, sounding dishonest through shaking cold and hunger, gave emphasis to the appearance. He shut the door, and quickly gained the street. At a small coal-shop he learnt that his mother was dead. The lad cried so bitterly that the woman-keeper of it gave him a crust of bread and some tea; but she was an upright woman, had heard of his going to gaol for stealing, and told him to clear off.

*   *   *   *   *   *

On a clear November midnight, a policeman on the bank of the Thames found a poor, ill-clad fellow, of some sixteen years of age, nearly dead with cold. The policeman took him to the station. A few days later, he might be seen using an axe in a philanthropic chip-yard where he fed and slept. Here Christian visitors took deep interest in the objects of their charity. And not a week passed without a visitor, and none visited the yard after the new boy's arrival without the shorn head attracting attention, exciting inquiry, receiving solution, and evoking advice.

"And who is this?" said a circular gentleman, of most agreeable manner and moderate attachment to the snuff-box, as he addressed the master. The story was given—begging and gaol!

"Well, my boy," said the kindly gentleman in a solemn tone, "it's a sad thing to break your country's law; all sin is against God; you must never do it again."

"But," interposed a second visitor, "did we not hear that he did it for his mother?"

"Yes, sir, I did," said the lad.

"Well, then, my boy, you were a brave fellow; I would have done the same. Cheer up! It is not every man who goes to prison who ought to go; Christ was in prison! Do your best, and I'll befriend you!"

Three months of gaol meditation on wrong done to him, that wrong now the reason for kicks from his own class and well-meant sermons, but not a word of sympathy, from Christians; these things had crushed the young lad. He was morose, gloomy, half-reckless. Is it not sometimes forgotten by those who wear the name of Christ, that He came 'not to condemn,' because He came to redeem? Lecturing degrades, sympathy elevates. In every grade and in every sphere—

"Men may o'erget delusion—not despair."

That moment that the lad felt another life in unison with his own, was the birth of hope—that frail yet majestic thing, that chief of conquerors.

"Tell me how he gets on," said this new friend, addressing the master, "and whether he is worthy of a better place, and he shall have it."

The lad was equal to the opportunity. Twelve months hence he was apprenticed to a skilled handicraft. Industry, night-school, Sabbath evening service, natural tact, and master's kindness made up his first few months in his new world. In very early days his wages were advanced; then he filled a post of some little responsibility, in which hard and brave endeavour found a worthy reward. Reasonable visions of the future were bright. Then it became known by the workmen with whom he was associated that he had been in gaol, and with this knowledge came the lad's greatest difficulty—the inevitable association of name and idea. Now, he had no character to sustain. His lot became unbearable to him. To render a reproof pungent, to account for aught missing, there was henceforth no difficulty. Suddenly he decamped. To his friend he said, in keenest despair, "I could do anything if men were like you."

He enlisted for a soldier. At the "Three Bells," the head-quarters of the enlisting officer, he was seen by a workman who sat soaking his brains in beer.

"That lad," said he to the sergeant, when the lad had gone out, "that lad's apprentice to a customer of mine. I suppose he's cut his sticks. They say as he's been in gaol."

At night, the sergeant, who had often been drunk, but had never been in gaol, asked, "What gaol were you in, old fellow?"

From business he had fled to be rid of that wretched spectre. It is at him again.

The maddened recruit absconded. He was captured, tried, and gaoled again. In a letter to this friend he said, "This is a damned world." . . .

But let us not miss the point of the case. Remember the unfortunate home, the kind disposition, the unlawful deed, the stern punishment, the bad name, the degraded lot, the efforts to rise, the stubborn opposition of common sentiment, the hopeless failure, the maddened despair, the flight. I am not able to follow the story of this hampered life further, but whatever else is open to doubt, is not this much clear, that the effect of gaol upon him was bad. As regards labour at least, all was disaster, no part was redeeming.

Every day in the police-courts of cities and villages, from

Land's End to John o' Groats, erring lads are being dealt with in like manner. . . .

But it may be asked, Do you imagine this case is a fair type of the cases which ordinarily find their way to gaol? To which I reply, as regards the boy, far from that. He is possessed of more elasticity of spirits, has finer ambitions, than lads who are born in the lowest ranks of life usually possess. But in this lies the strength of my case as regards the influence of gaol. For, having settled the point on the well-disposed and earnest, how much more have we settled it in the case of those who are not well-disposed and not earnest. If the influence of gaol is to-wards non-employment in the former case, will not ordinary experience justify our saying, *à fortiori*, so will it be in the latter case. B. Waugh. *The Gaol Cradle: Who Rocks It?* (1876), 29–34

4 W. D. Morrison Juvenile Offenders

The Rev W. D. Morrison (1852–1943), Chaplain of Wands-worth Prison from 1883 to 1898, is today regarded as one of the more percipient of the early criminologists (see G. D. Robin. 'Pioneers in Criminology: William Douglas Morri-son', *Journal of Criminal Law, Criminology and Police Science*, Vol lv [March 1964], 48). The extract below is from one of his two major books, *Juvenile Offenders* (1896), which became a standard work on the subject. Morrison was anxious to sug-gest improvements in the treatment of juvenile offenders, especially a reduction in the amount of imprisonment. He examines the causes of juvenile crime, finding much in society to promote delinquency.

When juveniles in work fall into the hands of the criminal law it is usually for offences such as assault, gambling, drunken-ness, malicious damage, obscene language, disorderly conduct, and so on. Nevertheless a certain percentage of juveniles in work are convicted of theft and embezzlement and sometimes of housebreaking and burglary. But the bulk of offences of this description, when committed by juveniles at all, are committed by juveniles out of employment. In short, occupation has the effect of altering the form which juvenile crime assumes; it has even the effect of diminishing its amount, but it has not the effect of totally abolishing crime. Adverse economic conditions are no doubt a potent factor in arousing and stimulating criminal desires, but it is a mistake to assume that crime is entirely a product of economic adversity. It is one among the many conditions which produce a criminal career, but it is not by any means the sole condition. Whilst denying the omnipotence of economic conditions in the production of juvenile crime, it must, on the other hand, be emphasised that economic remedies in the shape of steadier work and better wages would do a great deal towards reducing the proportions of juvenile offences against property. Moral life, like life as a whole, stands upon a material foundation, and if the virtues are not resting on a material basis in the form of steady work and adequate remuneration, they will be in most cases but poor and sickly plants. Of course instances exist of the absence of material blessings combined with purity and elevation of character, but these instances are exceptions which cannot be cited as standards for the ordinary man. The ordinary man—that is to say, the great mass of mankind—is deteriorated when placed under abnormal economic conditions. Adverse conditions of this kind prevent him from obtaining a proper amount of physical nourishment, and physical deterioration is often the prelude to mental degeneracy. Insufficient food, insufficient shelter, insufficient clothing, degrade men in their own eyes; they imagine, and not without reason, that they are objects of contempt to the community, and in many cases their conduct eventually falls to the same miserable level as their economic surroundings. This is more especially the case with the young. Juveniles in all ranks of life are exceedingly sensitive to public opinion, and unless gifted with great inborn force of character, are apt to become what the world in general considers them to be.

We shall now complete our examination of the economic

condition of juvenile offenders by endeavouring to show why three-fourths of them are out of work, or practically out of work, at the time of their arrest. The possession of work or the want of it is dependent upon two fundamental conditions—personal competence, and the state of trade. As a rule both these conditions operate simultaneously, and it is not very often that the loss of employment is produced by one of them alone. In depressed times it is the least efficient who are the first to lose work, and it is only on those rare occasions when an industry comes to a standstill that the thoroughly competent workman is thrown completely idle. In the ranks of labour the weakest, the most unfit industrially, are always the first to fall; the fittest, the most efficient, are always the last. In periods of great commercial prosperity almost any one can get something to do if he chooses to do it, but as soon as these exceptional circumstances begin to pass away the process of eliminating the least capable workers immediately and imperceptibly comes into operation. The least efficient are the first to be cast adrift; the class above them follows if trade depression deepens, and the process of sacrificing the less fit continues until trade commences to revive. All of us who are engaged in the task of procuring occupation for discharged prisoners are constantly being confronted with the operation of this law. A low standard of industrial ability, and therefore a considerable difficulty of obtaining employment or of keeping it when once obtained, is as great a drawback to the discharged prisoner as the condition of the labour market. In a very considerable number of cases the discharged prisoner is below the average in industrial capacity. Employers say that he is not worth his wages, that he is irregular in his habits, that he is unsteady, that he is not to be depended upon. In these circumstances it is not to be wondered at that the discharged prisoner should fall out of work as soon as the full tide of trade begins to recede. And when he loses work he falls back instinctively upon the criminal habits of the past.

What applies to offenders in general applies with equal force to the juvenile offender. He is out of work quite as much on account of industrial inefficiency as on account of the condition of trade. As a rule the juvenile offender has received little or no industrial training, as a rule he has not been accustomed to habits of regularity, in many cases his home surroundings are against him, and it often happens that he has not the physical strength for the only kind of labour he would otherwise be competent to perform. He accordingly belongs to the class of intermittent workers who are called in during emergencies, and are got rid of at the earliest possible moment. He has no permanent occupation, he drifts from one thing to another, and is in reality never in work in the sense of having some stable occupation at which he can count on earning a regular weekly wage. From what has already been said respecting the physical and parental condition of these juvenile offenders, it is perfectly plain that the industrial inefficiency which plays so large a part in making them what they are is in most cases outside their own control. W. D. Morrison. *Juvenile Offenders* (1896), 172–5

5 J. M. Rhodes London's Housing Problem

London's housing problem was as acute in the middle of the nineteenth century as it is today—see Thomas Wright's *The Great Unwashed, by The Journeyman Engineer* (1868), 126–50, for a well paid artisan's difficulties in this respect, and his account of the 'low' court in which he was forced to make his home. Certain parts of the metropolis were notorious as criminal areas (see Part Two), and those whom the housing problem forced into such places had little chance of emerging from them unscathed. The following tale appears in a number of publications of the late nineteenth century, being quoted from one to another. The dramatic language and the moralising tone should not blind us to the truth behind the story. (The police also had housing difficulties [27].)

They had been quietly turned out of their cottage. Where should they go? Of course to London, where work was thought to be plentiful. They had a little savings, and they thought they could get two decent rooms to live in. But the inexorable land question met them in London. They tried the decent courts for lodgings, and found that two rooms would cost 10s. per week. Food was dear and bad, water was bad, and in a short time their health suffered. Work was hard to get, and its wage was so low that they were soon in debt. They became more ill, and more despairing with the poisonous surroundings, the darkness, and the long hours of work, and they were driven forth to seek a cheaper lodging. They found it in a court I knew well, a hot-bed of crime and nameless horrors. In this they got a single room at a cruel rent, and work was more difficult for them to get now, as they came from a place of such bad repute, and they fell into the hands of those who sweat the last drop out of man, and woman, and child, for wages which are the food only of despair. And the darkness and the dirt, the bad food and the sickness, and the want of water, were worse than before; and the crowding and the companionship of the court robbed them of the last shade of self-respect. Then the drink demon seized upon them. Of course there was a public-house at both ends of the court. There they fled, one and all, for shelter, and warmth, and society, and forgetfulness. And they came out in deeper debt, with inflamed senses and burning brains, and with an unsatisfied craving for drink they would do anything to satiate. And in a few months the father was in prison, the wife dying, the son a criminal, and the daughters on the streets. J. M. Rhodes. *Pauperism, Past and Present*—read to Manchester Statistical Society (14 January 1891), 64

PART TWO

The Criminals

One central fact dominated nineteenth-century writing about crime—contemporaries were convinced of the existence of a separate criminal class, different in its ideas and behaviour from the honest poor. Modern writers who speak of the 'rough working-class' or who analyse criminal subcultures are dealing with essentially the same concepts, though of course in different and more sophisticated ways. The distinction made in the nineteenth century was not merely the familiar Victorian distinction between the deserving and the undeserving poor. We have already noted kindly comments on juvenile criminals from those who had seen much of them (see page 11), and the extracts that follow are often sympathetic and understanding in tone.

One particular aspect of the criminal class was the tendency of its members to congregate. The rookeries, the lowest housing districts, of London and the other large towns had within them smaller sections that had the reputation of being criminal areas. The concept of the criminal area is acceptable to modern criminological thought (for a recent discussion, see J. Mack. 'Full-time Miscreants, Delinquent Neighbourhoods and Criminal Networks', *British Journal of Sociology*, xv [1964], 38–53) and there is no doubt that in the nineteenth century several criminal areas could be identified (see the Penguin edition of J. J. Tobias, *Crime and Industrial Society in the Nineteenth Century* [1972]).

Of course, it is not possible to be sure how many criminals

there were in a particular street or how just it was to describe
that street as 'criminal'. Some contemporary opinions are just
wild generalisations. For example, though abundant evidence
was given before the Select Committees on Mendicity and on
Police in the metropolis in the years 1816–28, most of the witnesses were far from exact in their language. A representative of
a benevolent society clearly knew a great deal about Calmel
Buildings, Marylebone, and described in some detail the appal-
ling conditions in which over 700 people lived—nowhere else
had he met 'so much distress, so much profligacy, and so much
ignorance'. He went on to say, however, that 'we hardly ever
hear of a riot, or a murder, or burglary, in which several persons
are concerned, in which some of these poor creatures are not
implicated'. Again, while one can largely accept the testimony
of other benevolent workers that 'in the neighbourhood of
Shoreditch and Bethnal Green' was a group of thirty-five
families whose 150 members subsisted by 'begging and plunder',
while half the 2,000 people who lived in George Yard, Whitechapel, lived 'almost entirely by prostitution and beggary', the
use of hard figures should not blind us to the element of guess-
work in these conclusions. None the less, though individual
estimates and generalisations are suspect, the body of evidence
at least gives us the contemporary view. Moreover, it is not
uninformed opinion. Most of the witnesses were speaking of
conditions in small parts of London or other towns that were
well known to them personally, and many of them were directly
concerned with crime—stipendiary magistrates, police officers,
parish officials and the like.

6 W. H. Dixon London's Criminal Areas

Several accounts of the criminal areas were written in the
nineteenth century, often by clergymen or others sympathetic
to their inhabitants and familiar with their doings. The
journalists were also active in this field, of course, and this
description comes from the work of William Hepworth
Dixon (1821–79), a journalist and historical writer who was
editor of the *Athenaeum* from 1853 to 1869. In 1850 he wrote

a survey of London's prisons that included a consideration of the areas from which so many of their inhabitants came.

We take it for granted, that Clerkenwell is known to every breakfast table in this kingdom. To the careful reader of the police reports, the name of this district must be as familiar as the commonest household word. The constant conflict of its turbulent population with the guardians of the public peace, has given it a universal reputation. It is low London *of* low London. All great cities have their Clerkenwells. Manchester has its Deansgate; Liverpool its Waterloo-road; Nottingham its Marsh; Glasgow its Salt-market; Dublin its Liberty. The metropolitan district is only a type of one of the conditions of a town population, which prevails more or less intensely everywhere. It is the chief scene of violence and outrage which the capital has to boast. Although not so exclusively the haunt of thieves, burglars, prostitutes, and vagabonds, as St. Giles's and the low neighbourhoods about the Broadway, Westminster, it is, nevertheless, far more remarkable for crimes of the darkest kind than either of these notorious localities. . . .

Threading his way from Newgate, through Smithfield-market, along Cow-cross, and by Saffron-hill, into the heart of Clerkenwell, the pedestrian passes through some of the worst quarters of the great city. Some parts of this route lie through localities worse than the lowest parts of Paris; worse, perhaps, than the low haunts about the Canongate, in Edinburgh. He traverses narrow dirty streets and courts, crowded and filthy as the by-places in Houndsditch, miserable and destitute of light, water, almost of air; he sees property dilapidated and falling to a mass of foul and ugly rubbish; children with pale and ghastly faces; forms hideous with premature disease, arising from the unnatural and unhealthy circumstances into which they are helplessly cast. Of late years public attention has been drawn to this solid mass of misery, of low vice, of filth, fever, and crime. Respectability has become alarmed for its own safety. Unwelcome truths have been brought from these low regions of

vice and disease, to the comfortable homes and costly palaces
of luxury. By means of such agents as fever and cholera, the
mass of putrefying humanity has asserted its intimate connexion
with all other sorts of humanity breathing the self-same air, and
the misery has got to be looked at without eye-glasses. When the
truth was felt that white kid and Russian sables were no protection against the contagion of misery-made diseases, then
philanthropy began to flourish in high places. Field-lane and
Saffron-hill ceased to be thought picturesque. Men began to
pull down and rebuild. This work has proceeded somewhat, and
is now going on. God speed it! The new street, in continuation
of Farringdon-street, has opened up some clear vistas into the
former condition of the locality. Field-lane has been broken
into, and but a remnant of its former glory now remains;
enough, however, to enable one to understand what it must
have been in its palmier day. Let the inspector of the London
prisons—after emptying all his outer pockets, and buttoning up
his coat to secure his watch, pocket-book, and handkerchief—
penetrate this celebrated receptacle for stolen goods. The lane
is narrow enough for him to reach across from house to house,
and the buildings so lofty that a very bright sun is required to
send light to the surface. The dwellings on either side are dark;
in some of them candles or gas is burning all day long. The
stench is awful. Along the middle of the narrow lane runs a
gutter, into which every sort of poisonous liquid is poured.
This thoroughfare is occupied entirely by receivers of stolen
goods, which goods are openly spread out for sale. Here you
may *re*-purchase your own hat, boots, or umbrella; and, unless
you take especial precaution, you may have one of the impor-
tunate saleswomen—daughters of Israel, who are greater
adepts in the arts of cajolery than many of the fair ladies who
pique themselves on their success at charitable bazaars—
attempting to seduce you into the purchase of the very handkerchief which you had in your pocket at the entrance.

Let the observer emerge at the Clerkenwell end of Field-lane,
and then notice the character of the place he is in. Let him

pause for a moment to contemplate this *hot-bed of crime and demoralization.* Here is one of the great dunghills on which society rears criminals for the gallows, as on other dunghills it rears melons for the table. Look there, across the gap thrown open for the new street, at the sections which are laid bare—at the low, crowded dwellings, the broken windows, the tiles which have fallen out of their places, the dirt and haggard wretchedness which meet the eye at every turn. No wonder, indeed, to find a gaol in such a neighbourhood! The flavour of the fruit depends upon the quality of the soil: and here we have some of the richest rankness in the world. W. H. Dixon. *The London Prisons* (1850), 224–8

7 W. B. Neale and Thor Fredur   Low Lodging Houses

A feature of the criminal area was the low lodging house. The first of the following accounts was published in 1840, before the Common Lodging Houses Act of 1851 (14 and 15 Vict, c 28), under which police officers became inspectors of lodging houses. (Control had come to certain parts of the country a little earlier, by the Towns Improvement Clauses Act, 1847—10 and 11 Vict, c 34, sections 116–18—and the Public Health Act, 1848—11 and 12 Vict, c 63, section 66.) The passage written by Thor Fredur, however, published in 1879, shows that the controls could not eliminate all the evil features of the common lodging house. See also Charles Booth. *Life and Labour of the People in London,* Vol I (1891), 205–19

(a) W. B. Neale

Let the reader imagine himself introduced into a damp cellar, or dark and dirty garret, where he sees as many beds as it will hold, (from six to fourteen in number) ranged side by side, and closely adjoining one another; that in each of these beds he discovers from two to four persons, of either sex, and of all ages and character, who are, however, hidden from his view by the mass of clothes taken from those in bed, and now hanging on

B

lines in various directions about the apartment, and he will form some conception of the scene which a lodging-house at first view presents. Let him imagine that the temperature of this room is at a fever heat, owing to the total absence of all means of ventilation, and in consequence of so many persons breathing and being crowded together in so small a space; let him imagine himself assailed by a disgusting, faint, and sickening effluvia, to which the pure breath of heaven is a paradise, and he then may conceive the effects produced, on entering these crowded dormitories, by the vapour and steam floating about them. Let him remember that the bed-linen is rarely changed—once in six months—and that in these beds, meanwhile, have been located an ever changeful race of diseased and sick, as well as convalescent persons; and let him imagine these beds to be likewise visibly infested with all manner of vermin, and he will form a conception, far short however, of the reality of the horrible spectacle presented, not by one, but by many hundred lodging-houses in Manchester.

While, owing to the filthy state of these lodging-houses, juvenile offenders are generally found afflicted with scabies or itch, and the tinea capitis, or scald head, with a variety of other infectious diseases, it is here that they become familiarized with scenes of infamy offensive to every principle of morality; and here it is that they become initiated into every species of criminalty, by the precepts and example of adult and hardened offenders. The proprietors of these lodging-houses, and of the low beer and spirit shops, are the principal foils and receivers of stolen goods of the young delinquent; and hence these houses are always open to him, at times when his resources are low, as well as when he is flush of money. The juvenile delinquent, who is in general a gambler and a drunkard, is also a debtor, and usually behind-hand in his payment of the beer and the lodging-house keeper; hence, whatever sum he may plunder from the public, it goes to pay old scores, or is spent as fast as it is obtained upon his expensive passions; hence, while the delinquent in general finds the means of subsistence, either in plunder or

upon credit, he is, in a great measure, in the power of the pro-
prietor of the lodging-house, the spirit shop, or of that in which
stolen property is received—who, for indemnification of the
lodging, the food and liquor, or the money given in advance,
stimulate him to fresh plunder, the greater proportion of which
they find means of appropriating to themselves. . . .

Owing to the extent to which the system prevails among the
poor of sub-letting their houses to as many lodgers as it will
hold, or can be procured, they render the state of their dwellings, in point of physical comfort, little better and sometimes
worse than the common lodging-house.

Great as may be the increase of the means now afforded for
the detection of crime, by the organized Police Forces now
established through the kingdom, much of their efficacy in re-
pressing crime will be counteracted, until the Legislature
seriously takes in hand the important duty of breaking up the
principal haunts of infamy throughout the land—or at least,
until it places them under sanatory regulations, and the more
immediate and strict surveillance of the police. In the present
condition of things, the public are enormously taxed, in various
ways, for this neglect of the common duty of self-preservation
and of humanity. Were the ruling orders to pay that attention
which they are in duty bound, to improve the habitations and
thus promote the physical well-being of the poor, an immense
saving would speedily be effected to the public—crimes of every
kind would be lessened, especially frauds upon the mint and the
customs; there would be less to pay for pauperism, particularly that produced by sickness, and generated by the present
confinement and defective state in the ventilation and drainage
of the streets and houses inhabited by the poor. W. B. Neale.
Juvenile Delinquency in Manchester . . . (Manchester 1840), 53–5

(b) Thor Fredur

The common lodging-house is mostly situated in what may
be termed a predatory centre. It has a score of entrances and
exits—the greater number through windows and over walls;

but the latter are quite as easy of passage to those who know the places as the widest of its doors. Then it has hiding-holes in plenty. In short, a fugitive with the police hot after him could not do better than run to earth in such a place—that is, always supposing that he has made the night porter his friend. This being the case, and knowing the neighbourhood well towards the rear of the house, he would have no difficulty in obtaining entrance unseen at any time. Having done this, he might cut through the house and be off again, leaving those in chase hopelessly behind. Or he might take to the first vacant bed and lie still, thus baffling them as effectually. And in most instances the police would find the obstacles in the way of capture enormously increased by the fact that these abodes do not as a rule stand apart from one another, but in clusters. I could name right off a score of clusters of such houses, the individual edifices of which, opening in different streets, lie back to back; so that each cluster is really for some purposes only a single house. I have noticed men over and over again escaping from one of these houses through another.

Again, a man at issue with the law, taking up his residence in one of these houses, could defy its emissaries therein for any length of time, did he only take ordinary precautions. He could have his 'box', a coffin-like compartment containing a single bed, placed in a situation favourable to escape in the case of pursuit—standing in the midst of a number of complicated passages, with the choice of several pairs of stairs in case the occupier thought fit to fly by their means; and with a window opening out on to a roof over which he might make his way to any one of half-a-dozen different alleys in the neighbourhood. At the same time he would find nothing easier than to devise a signal whereby his friend the night porter could warn him in due time of approaching danger without anybody else being the wiser.

The night porter, too, is very useful to conveyancers of the Bardolph and Nym order. . . . Any time between one and five a.m. a peculiar knock will call the porter to one of the doors.

There a heavy parcel is thrust into his hand or flung into the passage, or he finds it deposited on the doorstep in an obscure corner. . . . Should he be at loss as to what to do with it he knows very well that a few hours will enlighten him on that point; and, thus enlightened, he has a hundred ways of getting rid of the thing at his ease. Should the bundle consist of clothes, he can have the things pawned article by article in twenty different pawnshops by as many different persons: for the crowds who frequent a common lodging house always include a number of men very willing to do a job of this kind at a moment's notice for a few pence. If the contents of the parcel have to be passed on to an ultimate receiver, it is easy to make them up into smaller packets, each of which can be despatched by different lodgers to their destination. There is no lodger who would refuse to do the night porter a service of this kind, for there is no knowing when he may not require a service at his hands in return. And matters are so managed that probably not one of the carriers has the smallest suspicion that he is 'aiding and abetting' a felony. Thor Fredur (J. Rutherford). *Sketches from Shady Places* (1879), 131–4

---

8 J. T. B. Beaumont   The Thieves' Public House

The thieves' public house was even more widespread than the common lodging house. This passage, written in the extravagant language of the early nineteenth century, describes a state of affairs that may well have existed for some time thereafter. It comes from a pamphlet written by John Thomas Barber Beaumont, managing director of the County Fire Office and a magistrate for Middlesex. He was an advocate of reform, particularly opposed to gin-shops, and was critical of the system of licensing operated by some of the magistrates of the metropolis, whom he accused of being under the influence of brewers. He was himself interested in the subject as an owner of land and of public houses. The nature of his work is indicated by its title: *A Letter to . . . Lord Sidmouth . . . shewing the Extreme Injustice to Individuals and Injury to the Public of the Present System of Public House Licensing.*

The horrid connection between the trades of thief-taking and thief-making has been so fatally proved, and also the instrumentality of flash-houses to that connection, that the *professional convenience* and advantage of these 'Preserves' must give way, I submit, to the public safety. My observations have long indicated flash-houses and cock and hen clubs to be the most effectual nurseries, academies, and houses of call for vices and crimes that can be devised. They administer to their victims' course, from their boyish seduction to their apprehension for the gallows. There the novitiate sees decency laughed to scorn and vice extolled as spirit; there each encourages the other to new expressions and acts of depravity; there thieves are brought together, and enabled to combine for extensive mischief; there inflamming liquors are at hand to drown reflection, and excite to deeds of fierceness; there, to crown the whole, innocent men are inveigled into the commission of crimes, by the agents of men whose duty it is to suppress crime, in order that money may be made by hanging them. All these evils have been suffered, because the thief-takers say if it were not for such houses we would not know where to find the thieves. Perhaps they might go a little further, and add—'If it were not for such houses we should not have any thieves to find!'

If thieves are proscribed from receiving liquor and entertainment in public-houses, they will not have their wonted opportunities to decoy new men into their ways, while, in the comparative solitude into which they will be driven, they will have leisure to reflect on the misery of their trade, and be furnished with motives to look out for a better. Street-walkers, prevented from artificially exciting their spirits at the numerous gin-shops open to them at every step, will be less likely to terrify by their yells and expressions, and to shock decency by their appearance. J. T. B. Beaumont. 'A Letter to Lord Sidmouth . . .', *The Pamphleteer*, Vol 9 (1817), 448–9

9 Fraser's Magazine   The Schoolmaster of Newgate

A long account of the criminal classes and their doings appeared in *Fraser's Magazine* in 1832 (Vols v and vi), under the title 'The Schoolmaster's Experiences in Newgate'. An extended version was published in book form in 1833, under the title *Old Bailey Experiences, Criminal Jurisprudence . . . by the Author of 'The Schoolmaster's Experiences in Newgate'*. The passage quoted here appears in both versions.

The term "desperate," as usually applied to these men, must not be taken in its common acceptation—bold, daring, absence of fear, and careless of personal danger. They are all, without exception, pusillanimous and rank cowards. The desperation they possess is that of a determined and inveterate gambler; they are ever employed in calculating the chances for and against them, in every unlawful adventure they think of embarking in; if they can but make the chances in their favour (that is, of escaping), they will unhesitatingly engage in any scheme or attempt at robbery. If, however, the commission of it be attended with the least possible risk of personal danger on the spot, they will always forego the adventure; and they have their exact odds in favour of every species of crime. The higher the game (they say), the less the risk. The high and safe game, however, requires a capital, as in the more honourable walks of life, to make an appearance—to move about with facility, and in what they denominate style. It is astonishing with what pleasure some of them will speak of the prospects they have of soon leaving off the dangerous walk of business they have followed, and embarking in that which brings more profit and less risk—each saying, "If I get off easy this time, I shall alter my game; I know I am a good workman, and ought to have been better employed." The character of one is the character of the whole class; their manners and notions are all of one pattern and mould, which is accounted for by their general acquaintance with each other, and their habits of association. They have a peculiar look of the eye, which may be known by any one much accustomed to see them; and the development of their features is strongly marked with the animal propensities. So very similar are their ideas and converse, that in a few minutes' conversation with any one of the party, I could always distinguish them, however artfully they might disguise themselves, and attempt to mislead me. They may be known almost by their very gait in the streets from other persons. Some of the boys have an approximation to the face of a monkey, so strikingly are they distinguished by this peculiarity. They form a distinct class of men by themselves, very carefully admitting noviciates into their secrets; he, however, who has graduated under one of their own approved body is unhesitatingly admitted into full confidence. He must, notwithstanding, prove himself acquainted with all the cramp terms peculiar to their craft, or he will still be considered "green," and not fit to be trusted. There is not one of the select who is not able to relate the whole history of any other individual in their body—how he first began, who first taught him, what he has done and suffered, &c. &c. They form one club, to whom all the *fences* are known (receivers of stolen goods), who will never purchase of a new hand without a proper introduction, for fear of "a *plant*" (being betrayed). An initiate is, in consequence, constrained to trust his spoils to some old offender, until he can himself become better acquainted, and gain confidence with the buyer.

In a recent work on Newgate,* there is mention made of a man who was in the habit of going to a house in Wingfield Street, Whitechapel, and shewing the boys large sums of money, and asking them to bring him goods to buy; from which it is understood he enticed them to commit crime. . . . It is a mistake to suppose he or any of his craft would go out to entice unknown persons to crime. The risk here is too great, and the parties too wary. . . . It is said, if there were no receivers, there would be no thieves; and the authorities have been advised to aim more at the buyer than the thief. That the receiver is as bad as the thief,

* Facts relating to the Punishment of Death in the Metropolis. Second Edition. By Edward Gibbon Wakefield, Esq. 1 vol. 8vo. Wilson.

must be admitted; but if it be resolved to a question of policy, I say, remove the thieves if you can, who will for ever, while they remain at liberty, make others, and annoy society. If, by any possibility, all the buyers of stolen goods could be annihilated, in twenty-four hours their places would be filled up by others embarking in the trade. The profits are too large, and the chances of detection too remote, until the thieves are removed, ever to blot them, as a class, out of society. Every regular thief let out upon the town draws into crime, in the course of one year, a dozen more, which continues the species; and this will ever be the case until the system at the Old Bailey be altered, where there really appears to be much more anxiety to take out of society casual offenders than the born and bred thief, whose whole life has been devoted to plunder. I have said they reckon all their chances: 1st, of their not being detected in the offence; 2dly, of their being acquitted; and 3dly, of coming off with what they call a small *fine* (short imprisonment). The only punishment they dread is transportation; they hold all others in contempt; and I believe even that of death would lose its terrors, did it not lead to the greatest of all their dreads, viz. transportation for life. Death, indeed, has no terrors for any one, until met with at close quarters. Tell the thief of death, and he will answer, "Never mind, I can die but once!" Name transportation, and he turns pale. This cannot be too strongly enforced on the presiding judges at the Old Bailey. Full three-fourths of the prisoners, every session, are determined offenders, all of whom are regardless of imprisonment for a short period. Their spirits enable them to surmount such trifles, when the prospect of again returning to liberty and enjoyment is not very remote. "Go along, time!" they cry; "only three months and a *teazing*. Never mind! that's over in ten minutes (meaning the flogging); I would take one for each month, if the *old fellow* (the judge) would let me off the imprisonment." *Fraser's Magazine*, Vol. v (June 1832), 522–3; *Old Bailey Experiences, Criminal Jurisprudence* . . . (1833), 39–43

10 S. Meredith   The Perils of Social Work

Many of the accounts of the criminal classes written by
people engaged in 'good works' betray a tendency to regard
them as creatures of a different species from the writer or
prospective readers. The following extract comes from one
such account; but it shows also the compassion with which
the poor were viewed, and the courage, both moral and
physical, needed for the social tasks so willingly undertaken.
It should be noted that Milly, the girl mentioned in the extract, became a devout Christian during an illness and died
young in a state of grace—which to the author of the passage
and many of her contemporary readers was far more important than any other fact about her, and was more than
adequate compensation for all her sufferings. The work
from which it is taken is a sympathetic account of efforts to
assist the criminal and other poor of London.

The place had no terrors for the lady. She had often passed
through its defiles before, without the least misgiving as to her
perfect safety. Milly was determined that this blissful state of
ignorance should exist no longer. She began immediately to try
to dispel it, in a manner that in ordinary cases would have
secured success.

"See, miss, don't rub so close to the butchers' shop-boards;
they'll say you've took off a piece of the meat, and will be having you in and searching you, and then, if they find nothing,
making you pay to be let out; and if you don't give in, making a
noise, and calling all the street around us."

This suggestion was sufficiently alarming to induce the lady
to walk in the middle of the passage, but to this Milly decidedly
objected.

"You mustn't do that, miss; it looks as if you was afraid, and
the moment *they* see it, *they*'ll take advantage of it."

"How so, Milly? What *can* they do, and who are 'they'?" she
questioned.

" 'What can they do' is it? Would you like to try? I can soon let you see; and who *they* are, too, *for I am one of them.*"

So saying, she grasped the lady round the waist, and lifted her up in her arms, and danced her like a baby, and, singing a hoarse lullaby, clasped her to her bosom. The struggles of the reluctant nurseling amused the bystanders, and even Milly was moved at her piteous cries, but only to mirth.

"You poor little thing," she said, "if my kindness would kill you, what would my other temper do?"

The court was astir. It was its time for gaiety. Women and men talked, laughed, and fought, with every variety of noise and attitude. Considerable attention was bestowed on Milly and her companion, although the majority seemed to be busy with affairs of their own. Short thin men, in very tight clothes, with caps fitting very closely to their heads, wandered restlessly about. Girls with dressed hair, and girls without dressed hair; girls in showy gowns, and girls in battered hats and bonnets. Old women, with old shawls wound round them, slipshod and beggarly in their manner, some poking in the channel, while they talked to a neighbour similarly employed, but seeking her treasure at the other side of the pavement. . . .

The lady noticed that she was being surrounded, and she anticipated some handling of a worse kind than that from which she had barely recovered.

Milly had a firm grasp of her arm, and though there was an attempt at being protective, sufficient evidence existed to prove that her power was not, by any means, exerted to procure liberation for the captive.

"Let us walk on, Milly," said the lady, in as courageous a tone as she could assume.

"Well, just to the end of the court," replied the victor; "and there you'll have to give me something to quieten these with,' pointing, as she spoke, to the people who were evidently interested in the affair.

"If you mean that I am to give you money," said the lady, "I can't; for I have not a single coin with me this moment."

"No money! no money!" cried Milly, in accents of utter astonishment, and, indeed, of complete unbelief. A lady without money was an idea she could not conceive. "Nonsense, miss, you'll just hand out something or other. It will be worse for you, if you don't. I won't be able to do anything to help you. *They'd* be on you like ferrits, and have it out of you in a minute. I'm your real friend, and will let you off easy. A few shillings will be enough to settle the matter between you and me; but *they*, though they take it so quiet-like, won't let you out of this alley until they have your purse, and anything else you may have in your pocket, without you now make a fair bargain with me. Ten shillings and your bag will satisfy me; but *they* will have your boots first thing, and then, maybe, your bonnet; and make you send home for any amount of money that they choose to ask. And, no doubt, you'll pay it, sooner than have it known that you come into such places as these to learn how sin is done."

The gravity of the situation appalled the lady, but she turned to her loving Saviour in silent prayer, and asked Him to undertake for her.

"Dear Lord Jesus," she prayed, "give me words to say to Milly that will be the means of saving her soul."

While she waited the answer to this prayer, expecting it in the form of a strong compulsion to explain the Gospel offer once more to Milly, and to add "line upon line, precept upon precept," to the frequent lessons that had been given her, she slowly and gently repeated the fact that she had "no money."

Milly angrily interrupted her, and said, "Well, miss, if you won't, I will;" and she dived into a mysterious pocket, and thence drew some coin which she presented to one of the men who were crowding round, saying, "There! Go along, and drink the lady's health."

With a sense of relief the captive saw them go into the public-house that occupied two-thirds of the enclosure, and she turned to her friend for an explanation of the scene.

"You would not believe me, miss, that it was dangerous to come down here this cold, wet evening. They want drink, and

they will have it; and you were a likely one to get it off of, with
your pockets full of money." . . .

By this time Milly and the lady had got through the narrow
passages, and passed between the posts that made the entrance
to them difficult, and were out in the thoroughfare, where
vehicles ply, and the world goes to and fro on all its affairs. . . .
Recently the courts and alleys where the foregoing matter took
place have been swept away by the metropolitan authorities, so
that no longer can "*they*" entrap and secrete passers-by, and
procure a price for their liberation. S. Meredith. *A Book about
Criminals* (1881), 63–8

11 Mary Carpenter   Schools and Juvenile Delinquents

Not all those who believed in the existence of a criminal class
or classes can be accused of taking a 'holier than thou' attitude. Miss Mary Carpenter (1807–77) was a leading member
of movements to provide schools for the children of the
poorest classes. Ragged schools were established in the
poorer parts of the town, and provided places where children
who would not be admitted elsewhere or would not go to
another school could receive an hour or two's instruction.
Miss Carpenter helped to found one of the first ragged
schools, in Bristol, in 1846. Reformatory schools were resi-
dential schools for youngsters who had committed crimes;
Miss Carpenter's book under that title in 1851 was one of the
early moves in the campaign to establish schools of this type,
and she opened one herself in 1852. This led to a movement
to establish what were called industrial schools, for those
children who were in danger of being drawn into crime but
had not yet committed an offence, and Miss Carpenter was
again active in their promotion.

The first passage illustrative of Miss Carpenter's thought
comes from her evidence to a Select Committee of the House
of Commons on Juvenile Offenders, and this is followed by
extracts from two of her more influential books. Together
they present this shrewd and informed observer's analysis of
the juvenile criminals of her day.

(a) Evidence to Select Committee on Juveniles, 1852

Question 799. Have you had much experience of the condition of the children of the lower classes, especially those who supply our criminal population?—During the last 17 years I have been in the habit of continually visiting the families of the lower classes of our population, especially the respectable labouring classes. I have also been in the habit of visiting their schools, and of attending to matters connected with these schools; during the last six years I have particularly directed my attention to the "perishing and dangerous classes," which are contemplated by the Ragged Schools. I have been very much struck with observing the strong line of demarcation which exists between the labouring and the "ragged" class; a line of demarcation not drawn by actual poverty, for I have found very great poverty in the children of the class connected with the higher schools I was just alluding to; far greater poverty than in the lower class. I should therefore consider that the line of demarcation consists in the utter want of control existing among the children of the lower class, and in the entire absence of effort on the part of the parents to provide proper education for their children. I believe that juvenile crime is entirely rising from the lowest class, and that in considering the provisions proper for the correction of juvenile crime, we must somewhat consider the conditions of the whole class. . . .

Question 815. Have any suggestions occurred to you as to the manner in which the lowest class can best be brought under school influence?—. . . I have noticed, in the progress of Ragged Schools, that by degrees the class attending them has become better than at first, that there are not nearly as many attending these schools of the directly vicious class. The master of our school considers that about one-third of the children in the school are connected, either directly or indirectly, with the criminal class; while fully two-thirds of the children outside this school, if not more, are directly connected with it. Therefore such a school as this cannot touch a certain class, and does not touch it. . . .

Question 816. Do you consider children convicted of felony or other dishonesty as forming a distinct class of themselves?—No, I should not consider them as forming a distinct class; that is, I do not consider that they are different in any respect from the bulk of the children whom I have been describing. I do not consider them at all worse in themselves. In the children of our school there are many who have been known for a length of time to be thieves, and who have been in the constant habit of pilfering. They have not been apprehended, it is true, but I do not consider them as worse after they have been apprehended than they were before, excepting only the brand which is attached to them by society. Some thieves, of course, may be considered as absolutely thievish by disposition; I believe that such are to be found in all classes of society. I know that they are found in the highest class, and amongst the labouring poor I know that they are continually found. But then they are treated differently from what they are in the lowest class. They are not exposed to prosecution; those on whom they have committed the theft feel that prosecuting them would place them in a degrading class, and therefore they try every means in order to avoid doing so; but in this lowest class, the moment a child is detected a thief he is prosecuted. I believe that if the criminal class of the lower part of the population were not placed in the circumstances in which they are, and were not exposed in the manner in which they are now, they would become different. . . . We never have a theft in the school; we never take any further precaution to protect our property than would be adopted in any other school; we believe that the children feel placed in a different position in respect to society when they are in the school. When they are out of school they are in a state of antagonism with society, and consider everything is lawful prey to them if they can but get it. When they are in school, they know and feel that they are under a bond of union with those who are trying to do them good, and therefore they do not feel tempted to steal. I believe this observation will be borne out by the experience of other Ragged Schools, more or less. *PP*, VII (1852), 97–102

(b) Reformatory Schools

That part of the community which we are to consider, consists of those who have not yet fallen into actual crime, but are almost certain from their ignorance, destitution, and the circumstances in which they are growing up, to do so, if a helping hand be not extended to raise them;—these form the *perishing classes*:—and of those who have already received the prison brand, or, if the mark has not been yet visibly set upon them, are notoriously living by plunder,—who unblushingly acknowledge that they can gain more for the support of themselves and their parents by stealing than by working,—whose hand is against every man, for they know not that any man is their brother;—these form the *dangerous classes*. Look at them in the streets, where, to the eye of the worldly man, they all appear the scum of the populace, fit only to be swept as vermin from the face of the earth;—see them in their homes, if such they have, squalid, filthy, and vicious, or pining and wretched with none to help, destined, it would seem, only to be carried off by some beneficent pestilence;— and you have no hesitation in acknowledging that these are indeed perishing and dangerous classes. Behold them when the hand of wisdom and of love has shown them a better way, and purified and softened their outward demeanour and their inner spirit, in Schools well adapted to themselves, and you hardly believe them to be separated by any distinct boundary from the children who frequent the National and the British Schools. Yet there is, and will long be, a very strongly defined line of separation between them, which must and ought to separate them, and which requires separate and distinct machinery and modes of operation.

In the present chapter an idea will first be given of the amount of crime among the juvenile portion of the population in our large cities; and it will be shown that this is co-existent in a great degree with absolute ignorance of the lowest kind, but still more with a striking deficiency in the nature of the education they have received. It will thus be proved that the present educational establishment for the labouring classes neither can nor will affect these perishing and dangerous ones, and that if we would effectually influence them, gratuitous ones of a different character must be provided for them. M. Carpenter. *Reformatory Schools for the Children of the Perishing and Dangerous Classes, and for Juvenile Offenders* (1851), 2–4

(c) Juvenile Delinquents

The *first class* consists of daring, hardened young offenders, who are already outlaws from society, caring for no law divine or human, perhaps knowing none; they live notoriously by plunder; their hand is against every man, and every man's hand is against them. . . . Such boys will generally be deemed incurable, from whom nothing is to be expected in after life, but to be a plague to society as long as they are at large. We need hardly ask what has been their previous history; it is certain that they have led an undisciplined childhood, over which no moral or religious influence has been shed, and which has been untrained to any useful, industrious habits. . . .

The *second class* is, if possible, more dangerous to society than the first, because more systematic in their life of fraud, and often less distinguishable by their external appearance and manner. These are youths who are regularly trained by their parents or others in courses of professed dishonesty, some as pickpockets, others as coiners, or in such varying modes of depriving their neighbour of his property as their peculiar circumstances may suggest. . . .

A *third class*, and perhaps a still more numerous one, consists of children who are not hardened and daring as the first, or *trained* to crime as the second, but who, from the culpable neglect of their parents, and an entire want of all religious or moral influence at home, have gradually acquired, while quite young, habits of petty thieving, which are connived at rather than punished by their parents, and which will, *unless effectually stopped*, lead ere long to daring violations of the law. . . . Into this class are thrown numbers who would seem to be led into dishonesty only by that love of enterprize and daring so common among boys of all classes; let them be actively employed, with their energies well exercised and directed, and there is no tendency to dishonesty in them, while the very spirit which led them into mischief will be developed for good. . . . In the higher classes of society, robberies of this kind committed by boys at school are deemed by many "capital jokes", "harmless pranks", "proofs of spirit"; in the lower ones, they subject a boy to imprisonment, even to transportation, the prison brand being fixed for life to the unfortunate children. . . .

In these three classes, actual destitution is scarcely even the alleged inciting cause of crime; if these children are poor, it is a poverty directly caused by vice. But our *fourth class* will consist of those who have been actually driven into crime by their utter destitution, by their being thrown on the world without any to care for them, while their claims on support from the National Poor Laws have been either passed by unnoticed or rejected by the administrators of those laws. . . .

Our *fifth class* live, both parents and children, in a condition of squalid poverty, and yet with a profession of gaining an honest livelihood, for they are hawkers, merchants of small wares, and indignantly repel any who should interfere with them, young as they are, in the exercise of their lawful calling. . . .

These children infest large towns; in the more agricultural districts of the south of England, there is a *sixth class* who seem to be born to a sort of hereditary calling, that of thieving. "We were born *travellers*", say two brothers under sentence of transportation; "my parents and two sisters are travellers now". This name cloaks every sort of vice; . . . though not so early trained in audacious thefts, and skilful evasion of detection as the town children, they grow up with an equally hardened wickedness of spirit, and become eventually bold housebreakers and robbers. . . . It is evident that children thus born and brought up can be rising to maturity only to perpetuate a distinct class in society ready for almost every species of crime.

M. Carpenter. *Juvenile Delinquents—Their Condition and Treatment* (1853), 23–33

---

12 The Criminal Trade

One useful—if not always reliable—source of information about nineteenth-century criminals is provided by the autobiographical accounts of the gentlemen (in the nineteenth-century sense of the term) who served sentences of imprisonment. Edward Gibbon Wakefield (1796–1862) used his prison experiences (he was sentenced to three years' imprisonment in 1828 for abducting an heiress) as the basis for discussions of public policy on criminal matters—his *Facts Relating to the Punishment of Death in the Metropolis* of 1831 is given credit for helping in the campaign to reform the criminal law. Others were content merely to describe their experiences, and the following extract is from a typical work. In the form of a rather stilted conversation, the author presents a description of some varieties of the criminal trade.

"Harry," I asked, "what's that bloke'* here for, who occupies the end bed?"

"Twineing."

"Twineing! What's that?"

"Don't you know that yet? why you must be a greenhorn not to know that. Well! I'll tell you. Suppose you start in the morning with a good sovereign and a '*snyde*'† half-sovereign in your pocket; you go into some place or other, and ask for change of the sovereign, or you order some beer and give the sovereign in payment; it's likely you will get half-a-sovereign and silver back in change. Then is the time to 'twine.' You change your mind, after you have 'rung'‡ your snyde half 'quid'§ with the good one, and throwing down the 'snyde' half, say you prefer silver; the landlord or landlady, or whoever it is, will pick up the snyde half-quid, thinking of course it is the same one they had given you!"

* Man. † Counterfeit. ‡ Substituted. § Sovereign.

"Is that a good game, do you think?" . . .

"If he can manage to begin every morning with yellow stuff, he may make a couple of 'quid' a day; but if he can only muster white stuff, why of course he can't make so much." . . .

"I have heard you speak of 'hoisting,' how do you go about that?"

"Ah! that's a much better game, but it requires a fellow to be rigged out like a 'toff,'* and they generally have a 'flash moll,'† with them at that job. She can secrete articles about her dress when in a shop looking at things, and that's one way of 'hoisting.' Jewellers' shops are the best places for that game. I know a bloke who made several hundreds at it; he took fine lodgings, and his moll looked quite the lady, so he orders some jewellery to be sent on sight; he prigs the best of it and bolts. Then you can get snyde jewellery made to look the same as real stuff, and when you are in the shop with your moll, she is trying on a ring perhaps, when you put the snyde one in its place and she sticks to the right one."

"I am afraid that game would be above my abilities?"

'Well, I'll tell you what I did once, and what you may do when you get out, when winter sets in; you can have some other game in summer, perhaps go hawking, and do a bit of thieving when you see the coast clear. My brother and I and another bloke went out 'chance screwing,' one winter, and we averaged three pounds a night each. My brother had a spring cart and a fast trotting horse, so when it began to grow dark, off we set to the outskirts of London. I did the screwing in this way. Wherever I saw a lobby lighted with gas, I looked in at the key-hole. If I saw anything worth lifting I 'screwed' the door— I'll teach you how to do it—seized the things, into the cart with them, and off to the next place." . . .

"A 'highflyer' is a bloke who dresses like a clergyman, or some gentleman. He must be educated, for his game is to know all the nobility and gentry, and visit them with got-up letters, and that kind of thing, for the purpose of getting subscriptions

---

* Gentleman.   † Prostitute of the gayest sort.

to some scheme. A church-building or missionary affair is the best game. There is only one good 'highflyer' in the prison. I knew him get 150*l.* from a gentleman in Devonshire once, and he thinks nothing of getting 30*l.* of a morning." . . .

"Macing means taking an office, getting goods sent to it, and then 'bolting' with them; or getting goods sent to your lodgings and then removing. I'll tell you a game that you might try now and again as you have a chance, and that is 'fawney dropping,' you know 'fawney' means a ring. Well, you must have a 'pal,' and give him a 'snyde' ring with a ticket and the price marked on it. When you are walking along the street and see a likely 'toff' to buy the ring, your 'pal' goes on before and drops it, you come up behind him, and in front of the gentleman you pick up the ring, which is ticketed, say five pounds. Well, you turn to the 'toff' and say to him that you have found a ring which is entirely useless to you, as you never wear these articles, and ask him to purchase it. He will most likely look at the ticket, and see it marked five pounds, and if you say you will let him have it for three pounds, or two pounds, or even for one pound, if he hesitates, it is also likely he will buy it, thinking he is getting a great bargain."

"What do you mean by 'snow-dropping?' " I asked.

"Oh!" said he, "that's a poor game. It means lifting clothes off the bleaching line, or hedges. Needy mizzlers, mumpers, shallow-blokes, and flats may carry it on, but it's too low and paltry for you."

"Who do you mean by mumpers and shallow-blokes?" I enquired.

"Why 'mumpers' are cadgers; beggars in fact. . . .

"I spoke of 'snotter-hauling.' Although I think you are too old for that 'racket'—and unless you were very hard up and in a crowd, I would not bother about it. It would not pay for the risk run. It does best for 'kids.'* A little boy can sneak behind a 'toff' and relieve him of his 'wipe' as easily as possible. I know a little fellow who used to make seven 'bob' a-day at it on the

* Boys.

average; but there were more silk 'wipes' used then than there are now."

"What do you mean by 'lob-sneaking,' and 'Peter-screwing?' "

"Why, 'lob' means the till, and 'Peter' means a safe. Stealing the till and opening the safe is what we call "lob-sneaking and Peter-screwing.""

"And what is 'jumping' and 'jilting?' "

" 'Jumping' is getting into a house through the window; and 'jilting' is getting in on the sly, or on false pretences at the door, and sneaking what you can find. It's not a bad game to go into hotels, for instance, as a traveller, and as soon as you see a chance to sneak anything, to bolt with it. I know some fellows who make a fair living in this way."

"Then there is 'twisting' and 'fencing?' "

"When you go into any place where hats, coats, or umbrellas are left in the lobby, you can take a new 'tog,' or a new hat, by mistake for your own. That is 'twisting,' or ringing the changes. Then the 'fence-master' is the fellow who buys stolen property. I will give you the names of some of these blokes in London before you go out. You must know where to dispose of a 'super,'* or whatever you get, or it would be of no use to you. You know what 'buzzing,' or pocket-picking is, of course; and you have heard of working on the 'stop,' most likely. Which means picking pockets when the party is standing still; but it is more difficult on the 'fly.' You must remember that. I remember once going along Oxford Street, and I prigged an old woman's 'poke,'† on the 'fly.' She missed it very quick, and was coming after me when I slipped it into an old countryman's pocket as I was passing. She came up and accused me with stealing her purse. I, of course, allowed her to search me, and asked her to fetch a 'bobby,' if she was not satisfied. Well, I followed the old countryman and accused him of stealing my purse. And, my Crikey! if you had only seen how the old codger looked when he found the purse in his pocket. I threatened to give him in

* Watch.　　† Purse.

charge of the first 'copper' I saw; and he was so frightened that I actually got a 'quid' out of him to let me off."

"Well now, tell me about 'snyde-pitching.' "

"Snyde, you know, means counterfeit or bad, anything bad we call snydey. Snyde-pitching is passing bad money; and is a capital racket, especially if you can get rid of 'fins.' "

"What are 'fins.' "

"Five pound notes, or flash notes. I can give you the address of one or two fellows who make bad coins, and you can pass one or two when you see a fair chance."

"What do they charge for sovereigns, for instance?"

"The charge depends on the quality, you can get them at from six to fifteen shillings. Those at fifteen shillings no one can discover. They are the weight, the size, and all that is required. The low-priced ones of course you must run more risk with. Making bad coins is one of the best games out, and you can carry it on with less risk. For instance you can have your place where you work so blocked up that before anyone can enter, you will have time to destroy all your dies and tools; and melt or 'plant' your metal, and without them they cannot convict you. I know a bloke in Birmingham now, who was getting up Scotch one pound notes when I was 'copt,' and he is a capital hand at the trade. He once made a good deal by making snyde postage stamps." . . .

"The other day I heard a bloke talking about a 'picking-up moll' he used to live with. What did he mean by that?"

"O! that's a very common racket. He meant a 'flash-tail,' or prostitute who goes about the streets at nights trying to pick up 'toffs.' When she manages to do this her accomplice the cosh-man (a man who carries a 'cosh' or life preserver) comes up, when she has signed to him that she has got the 'toff's' watch and chain, and quarrels with him for meddling with his wife. Whilst the quarrel is going on the moll walks off with the booty. I know one coshman who pretends to be a missionary, and wears a white choker. Instead of quarrelling, he talks seriously to the 'toff' about the sin of fornication, and advises him to pursue a more becoming life in future, and finishes off by giving him a religious tract!"

"Now I have nearly finished my questions, but whilst there is time tell me about 'magging,' and 'mag-flying.' "

"Magging is not so good a game as it used to be. It means more particularly, swindling a greenhorn out of his cash by the mere gift of the gab. You know if it were not for the flats, how could the sharps live? You can 'mag' a man at any time you are playing cards or at billiards, and in various other ways. As for 'mag-flying,' that is not good for much. You have seen those blokes at fairs and races, throwing up coppers, or playing at pitch and toss? Well these are 'mag-flyers.' The way they do it is to have a penny with two heads or two tails on it, which they call a 'grey,' and of course they can easily dupe flats from the country." . . .

"Well then tell me about 'locusing,' and 'bellowsing.' "

"Locusing is putting a chap to sleep with chloroform, and bellowsing is putting his light out. In other words, drugging and murder."

"Now then, shew me how to hang a fellow up, or put the 'flimp' on him, as you call it."

"D'ye see that bone in the wrist? Just get that on the wind-pipe—so," (shewing me practically how to garrot). *Five Years' Penal Servitude, by One Who has Endured It* (1878), 66–78

---

13 G. C. Chesterton Housebreakers' Tools

One pioneering criminological investigation was the work of the Royal Commission on a Constabulary Force, appointed in 1836. The Commission had three members, Charles Shaw Lefevre (1794–1888), MP, Speaker of the House of Commons 1839–57; Colonel Charles Rowan (?1782–1852), CB, a soldier who was Commissioner of Police for the Metropolis 1829–50; and Edwin Chadwick (1800–90), the famous reformer. Samuel Redgrave (19) was secretary. The Commission's papers make it clear that Edwin Chadwick did most of the work.

The Commission's *First Report* was published in 1839, and served many subsequent writers as a quarry from which to dig out material, often without acknowledgement—even the great Henry Mayhew was not immune from this. There was no other report—when Chadwick wrote to the Home Secretary suggesting a further investigation, he received a dusty answer. The Commission's work is here represented by two extracts. The first is taken from a description of the criminal classes and their methods of work, written for the Commission by G. C. Chesterton, Governor of the House of Correction of Westminster, and printed as an appendix to the *Report*.

The tools used in house-breaking vary according to the nature of the robbery; experienced burglars make their own as greater security; some of the most celebrated men in the line have been smiths or Birmingham and Sheffield manufacturers. The following are more or less required at every crack (burglary): Crow-bar, centre-bit, lantern, keys, picklocks, saw, pistol, pocket-knife, nux vomica or prussic acid. A short description of these instruments will be necessary properly to understand their use. The crow-bar is constructed on a similar principle to that in common use; they are of two sizes, one for the pocket, and a larger one; one end is made chisel-like, and the other curved; its use is to wrench open doors of every description, when noise is not of much importance. . . .

The centre-bit is a very essential instrument; it is made upon a small scale, the stock being formed to separate into pieces for the pocket; its use is termed panelling; holes are bored along the edge of the style of a door, within half an inch of the bead of the panel, a pocket-knife is then run along from hole to hole, the panel is removed, and then entrance is effected. . . .

Keys and picklocks are always in requisition, either to gain an entrance into a house, or after the entry is effected. . . .

The saw is used in cases where the lock or bolt is so strong as not to be strained by the force of the crow-bar; a hole is bored through the door, just above the lock, with the centre-bit, a key-hole saw is introduced, and the piece of the door upon which the lock is fixed is cut entirely away.

Pistols are now and then taken to burglaries, where the risk is great, where the expected booty is considerable, and where the parties concerned are well aware that, should apprehension take place, they, from a previous conviction, stand the chance of being hanged; but burglars know the dangerous ground on which they stand when brought to the bar on a charge of house-breaking if deadly weapons have been found in their possession; they therefore avoid carrying them as much as possible. It occasionally happens that a single party sleeps on the premises where a burglary is intended; in such cases a pistol is necessary, one of the party being placed at the bedside of the sleeper, pistol in hand, to prevent any disturbance from that quarter. . . .

Nux vomica, commonly called hog's or ox vomit and prussic acid are chiefly made use of to destroy animals of the canine species, which might disturb them by giving mouth. *PP*, XIX (1839), 218–19

_____

14 Edwin Chadwick The Royal Commission's Questionnaire

The Royal Commission on a Constabulary Force, like all investigations with which Edwin Chadwick was concerned, was a pioneer of method. Lengthy questionnaires were drawn up, some for answer by magistrates, members of watch committees or boards of guardians, and others for answer by prisoners. The following extract is from the questionnaire for prisoners, and the questions quoted give an indication of the type of information sought. Ellen Reece was in Salford Gaol in 1837, and her answers were recorded for her by the Chaplain. She had been sentenced to fourteen years' transportation for stealing money, and in April 1838 she was sent to New South Wales. The only other information about her fate is that in 1846 she was given permission to marry a man who had been sent out to the Colony as a convict twenty years previously, and that he was killed in an accident eighteen months after the marriage. Ellen's description of her life is supported by similar answers from other girls who answered questionnaires at the same time, and by the case-histories published in 1853 by the then Chaplain of the same prison, the Rev H. S. Joseph, in his *Memoirs of Convicted Prisoners*.

---

1. *What is your name, age, and the offence for which you are in prison?* Ellen Reece—24—Felony—Born in Wales.

2. *Are you single, married, or a widower? Have you children—how many?* Single.

3. *What has been your calling, or occupation?* Domestic Servant for six months at about 16 years of age.

4. *Are your Parents living? If not, what was your age when they or either of them died?* Mother is living. Father died when she was 13.

5. *If either Father or Mother be dead, has the survivor married again? If so, how long ago?* Mother still a Widow—out of 18 children only Ellen and two older alive. Sister 29—Brother 28 both respectable, most died young.

6. *Are you illegitimate? or a foundling?* Legitimate.

7. *Where were you brought up? At the house of your Parents or at that of any other relation or friend? or in the workhouse, or in the streets, being left without care and contronl?* Was brought up by Parents 'till 14.

8. *Of what calling were your Parents? Did they, or either of them, continue long in any service?* Father was a Slap-dasher—Mother kept house—Father worked for himself.

9. *Of what character was your Father? Was he honest, industrious and sober?* Was honest and industrious, but fond of drink.

10. *Of what character was your Mother? Was she honest, virtuous, industrious, and sober?* Mother was all these.

11. *Did your Parents regularly attend a place of worship, and require you to accompany them?* Yes, the Welch Independents. They always saw her to School every Sunday—Mr Roby's an Independent Sunday School.

12. *What care was taken of you by your Parents? Did you ever run away from them? What induced you to do so? Were you punished for do-*

ing so; and in what way? 'The greatest care as could be took of a child'. First ran away from home 6 months after Father's death then between 13 and 14, took some of her clothes and pawned them at a neighbours, said her Mother wanted to make rent up. Got 11/– and went away without any object, met a Girl who had stolen some Clothes who asked her to go with her to pawn them, she got a good deal and she took Reece to a cellar in Shudehill where were about 9 young Girls younger than herself, not for prostitution but to watch people out of their houses and commit thefts—no men went there. Mother found her after 3 days, took her home, beat her with a rod for ¼ hour. In a month Mother got her a place at Miss Clayton's at 1/– a week and food there 3 months. A Girl came begging (about 19) she gave her food out of the window—2 days after came again and then the Girl persuaded her to run away with her to go to her Aunts. She took her with her bundle to a house, where was a Gentleman waiting, at Mrs Porters, a bad house in Chapel Walks, now pulled down and she keeps a bad house in Mason Street Portland Street 4 or 5 girls now—one of the first common houses. He made her tipsy—did not know what was done or where she was when she found herself next morning alone—4 sovereigns left for her by him—ill for 2 days in Bed. There about a week—would not stay. Went out with one of the Girls and gave her the slip. Met with Margaret Axon aged 14, since transported from Liverpool and went Shoplifting with her for 12 months. Mother never knew where she was. At the end of 12 months Mother met her again, took her home and beat her very severely with a rope, took her clothes and locked her up 4 days on bread and water. Then after 2 months got her another place at Mr Johnson's, a public house in Old Garratt. 2/– a week. Mistress very kind to her, took her to a place of worship, R.C. Chapel in the afternoon for 6 months. One of the children had lost its beads and she dared not go home. Ran away and got to Shoplifting again for some months, till one night two others Jane Storey and Anne Storey and Reece broke into her late Masters house between 1 and 2 in the morning and stole as much apparel as raised 18/- had had nothing to eat for a day and half and went first to the Pantry the dog knew her and did not offer to bark. She was met in the Street about a month after by the Brewer who recognised her Gown and promised if she would go with him he would not tell. She refused and he kept hold of her. She was committed for Sessions and got 1 month. The Chaplain got her restored to her Mother. She stayed at home 3 months, Mother used her kindly; then went off Shoplifting and never home again.

13. *Did the occupation of either of your Parents necessarily take them from home?* Mother sold Eggs and took in Lodgers.

14. *Did you attend school? If so, for how long, and at what description of school; whether Dame School, National School, British and Foreign School, Sunday School, Church School, or Dissenting School?* 5½ years at Independent School 3 years at the National School paid 1d. a week.

15. *Were you taught to read and write?* Taught to read and write at National School.

16. *Can you now read and write? . . .* Can read well and write tolerably. Understands generally what she reads. Never fond of reading—— Read more in prison than anywhere else. . . .

23. *What were your condition and habits immediately before entering upon dishonest courses? Were you addicted to the use of spirituous liquors?* Was an orderly good Girl not given at all to liquor. Was very obstinate and often got a cuffing—did not like it and wished to be her own mistress.

24. *What was the immediate cause of your first offence? Whether to procure any particular gratification, and of what kind? From sudden temptation, or opportunity; if so, of what kind? Or from distress; if so, state the nature and cause of the distress; whether from imprudence or other misconduct?* About 2 days before she went her mother boxed her, and she said to herself, "She was old enough to take care of herself without being beat". Kept getting her things by degrees and then went off. Did not know whether to turn back or not—heart filled.

25. *What circumstances induced you to commit other offences?* I did

not like to work and therefore must steal to maintain myself. "When I left home did not mean to work any more at all." . . .

30. *When not in honest employ how were you maintained? If by depredations, describe their number, nature, and mode of committing them?* Shoplifting—Bad Houses. Generally went two together Shoplifting—method was to go into a linen drapers shop, first rate shops, and ask to see linen at such a price. Ask for Lutestring and take a bit for a pattern, take a yard of lutestring and 2 or 3 yards of linen, then ask for Stockings, Gloves, Handkerchiefs, and when a good many things on the counter, so that they did not know the Count of them, when the back was turned to reach something else, to slip them under their shawl; sometimes into a large square fustian pocket fastened round the waist and hanging nearly to the knees. This is not a very common thing—she and Margaret Axon (who is transported) made it out themselves. Paid for the small articles and walked out gently and made away as fast as they could to Newton Lane; a person of the name of Thompson who kept a private house in Thompson Street Newton Lane, he was what is called "a Fence" he was taken up 3 years ago transported for 14 years. After he was gone could not find anyone else to take 'em and thought it dangerous to go to pawnbrokers, so gave over Shoplifting and took entirely to the Streets and robbing Mens pockets. Made a deal of money Shoplifting, made £1 each in the day. . . . She did not become a regular prostitute 'till Shoplifting failed—was miserable both ways, but going on the Streets was most profitable. . . . Most Girls will rob by violence and especially drunken men. She did not like to see a man abused who had been robbed. Once heard of a girl taking £800, Jane Corry, but she was discharged. . . .

32. *In what way did you elude detection, pursuit, or apprehension? In what manner did you ever escape, or were you let off, after the apprehension?* Getting out of the way as soon as possible—slowly at first and then run when out of sight. Sometimes changed a Dress after a robbery. Often taken to watch-house and dare say has been let off 20 times because nothing found on her.

33. *How often have you been apprehended?* More than she can remember. Thinks been in Gaol about 14 times and once in Liverpool—was 2 years at Liverpool, on the Streets.

34. *How often have you been convicted?* This is the 3rd conviction —First 1 month, 2nd 6 months, 3rd discharge, 4th transported, and once discharged at Liverpool Sessions. . . .

39. *Were your practices and pursuits in any and what way influenced by fear of the Constables?* Was always afraid of them. They were scarcely ever away from the house.

40. *Were you or any of your associates in crime known to the Constables?* Well known—and my Companions—only as bad characters.

41. *Did you or any of your companions associate with the Constables, and if so, to what extent?* Neither herself, nor any of her Companions.

42. *Did you or they use any means with the Constables, either to distract their attention, or induce them to permit or facilitate your escape? If so, of what kind?* Girls would have hiding places in dark situations, taking a brick out, or putting it amongst rubbish. Frequently leaving town for a while, I should have gone this time on Monday to Liverpool, having done the robbery (£34) on the Saturday. I might have stopped there 12 months. A deal of girls live with their parents and maintain the whole family, these make the most money of any, for the police don't know them only seeing them at night; they don't see them in the bad houses. Such go to Mrs Morts and Matthews, but will not go to a house if they can help it; to some back Street. Gentlemen notice the features so much better when you go to a house. They are literally "deeds of darkness". Chadwick Papers (12), University College, London

15 **William Augustus Miles**   **Poverty, Mendicity and Crime**

William Augustus Miles was employed on at least two official enquiries into crime and criminals. He presented a report to the Select Committee of the House of Lords on the

Gaols in 1835 (see *PP*, XI [1835], 581, and XII [1835], 177, 246, and 387). He also spent some time making enquiries in the north on behalf of the Royal Commission on a Constabulary Force (see page 56). In January and February 1837 Miles travelled from Chester on a circular route that took him through much of Cheshire and Lancashire. He sent back a constant stream of reports to Chadwick, together with witnesses' statements. Much of his material is reflected in the Commission's report, and some of it was reprinted, together with his main report to the Gaols Committee of 1835, in the work from which the following extract comes. His notes are—not unnaturally—unsystematic, and he probably placed too great a reliance on what he was told by prison officials, police officers and criminals. Yet this latter fault is something of a virtue from our point of view, for it caused him, or so it seems, to write down stories very much as they came from those who talked to him. (This characteristic of recording his respondent's own words is of course one of the features of Henry Mayhew's work that endears it to posterity.) When Miles records that a prisoner told him '—, of Berwick Street, a pawnbroker, takes the greatest number of silk handkerchieves; knows them to be stolen . . . banters the boys when examining the goods, and says, *"Cheapside ones*, eh!" '—one feels that the speaker is coming very much alive.

Westminster Bridewell

D. Ward, aged 17, No. 8 on the prison list, a young burglar, four times in prison before.

Is in prison for breaking a window with an intention to steal; has been a thief ever since he was 10 years old; works with men who take the property he steals, they always go together. About three years ago, he stole a piece of raw silk out of a carriage, the men fenced it for £60, his share was £19, the money lasted about a fortnight. . . . Four years ago was tried for his life, for stealing silk crepe shawls, was condemned but got off with a year at Cold Bath Fields.

He never takes a handkerchief, the men who go with him take watches sometimes, to take a man's watch is to 'flimp him', it can only be done in a crowd, one gets behind and pushes him in the back, while the other in front is robbing him. . . . He was detected starring a jeweller's window, at Hoxton, had about £200 worth of goods in his hand when seized, the men escaped. . . .

G. Smith, No. 12, aged 12.

Steals check braces from carriages, for which he gets 1s. a pair; can get three or four of an evening, takes them to Buckeridge Street, St Giles, where he meets a man who buys them, or any other article of saddlery. . . .

J. Kennedy, a pickpocket, 17 years old, in once before.

Does not steal handkerchiefs, they are not worth his notice; other boys take them: he only takes purses; he works for Nelson; three go together; two 'stall' while the other 'buzzes'; they share and share alike; if he finds any 'finnips' (£5 notes) in the skin or purse, he gives them to Nelson to fence. Nelson gets from £4 to £4.10s. for them; the richest purse he ever took was £20; after a good haul, a boy can afford to lay by for a day or two; the time to work is from 1 to 6 o'clock. . . .

William Holland, No. 16, aged 17, has been in prison six times before.

He has been a pickpocket three years. . . .

It is dangerous to keep a stolen note in possession, and they get rid of it as quickly as possible. Gold they keep, as it cannot be identified.

Some of the girls at Milberry's, pickpockets at night, while one talks to the man, the other robs him; but they are not dexterous, *they pull it out all of a flare*. The boys will not teach them; they would lose their trade if the girls were to become expert. He never trusts to girls; they ought not to be trusted, if a thief wishes to be safe. . . .

He has worked for Nelson; quarrelled with him about a share of booty. Nelson is the most expert pickpocket about town. Works in Regent Street, Bond Street, Piccadilly, and St

C

James's Street; he took one day in Piccadilly, between the hours of 1 and 6, purses containing to the amount of £25.

He is generally, indeed always attended by younger boys, who rob whilst he screens them, or calls off attention. He was once pursued, and swallowed three sovereigns.

Nelson watches at Granger's, and similar shops, to see where gentlemen put their purses; then gives a signal to his underling across the street, who comes over to do his work, under the shelter of Nelson, who he says has followed the line 10 years. . . .

Night is the best time for handkerchiefs; he never makes less than 30s. a week, from that to £6, and sometimes much more. This was his first season at purses, and he could always be sure of obtaining as much as £8 a week by them. H. Brandon (ed). *Poverty, Mendicity and Crime* . . . (1839), 111–15

✓ **16 Charles Dickens and Arthur Morrison Through the Eyes of the Novelist**

The novelist has the gift of making his characters live for us, and this is a useful method of deepening our knowledge of the people of the past, if we can be sure that the picture presented is accurate—as the following passages are. It is true that Charles Dickens did a little violence to reality in *Oliver Twist* —for the sake of the plot, Oliver had to be dragged into the gang and Noah Claypole given access to it much more promptly than in real life, where there was competition for entry to a high-class group like Fagin's—but when he shows us the criminals in their natural habitat his accuracy can be proved from numerous sources. Arthur Morrison was writing half a century later than Dickens (*Oliver Twist* appeared in 1837–8, *A Child of the Jago* in 1896) but there is a timelessness about his picture of the receiver at work that makes it valid for the nineteenth century as a whole. Again there is independent testimony to its accuracy.

(a) *Field Lane*

A dirtier or more wretched place he [Oliver] had never seen.

The street was very narrow and muddy, and the air was impregnated with filthy odours. There were a good many small shops; but the only stock in trade appeared to be heaps of children, who, even at that time of night, were crawling in and out at the doors, or screaming from the inside. The sole places that seemed to prosper amid the general blight of the place, were the public-houses; and in them, the lowest orders of Irish were wrangling with might and main. Covered ways and yards, which here and there diverged from the main street, disclosed little knots of houses, where drunken men and women were positively wallowing in filth; and from several of the doorways, great ill-looking fellows were cautiously emerging: bound, to all appearance, on not very well disposed or harmless errands. . . .

Near the top on which Snow Hill and Holborn Hill meet, there opens, upon the right hand as you come out of the City, a narrow and dismal alley leading to Saffron Hill. In its filthy shops are exposed for sale huge bunches of second-hand silk handkerchiefs, of all sizes and patterns; for here reside the traders who purchase them from pickpockets. Hundreds of these handkerchiefs hang dangling from pegs outside the windows or flaunting from the door-posts; and the shelves, within, are piled with them. Confined as the limits of Field Lane are, it . . . is a commercial colony of itself: the emporium of petty larceny: visited at early morning, and setting-in of dusk, by silent merchants, who traffic in dark back-parlours, and who go as strangely as they come. Here, the clothesman, the shoe-vamper, and the rag-merchant, display their goods, as sign-boards to the petty thief.

(b) *The Artful Dodger*

He was a snub-nosed, flat-browed, common-faced boy enough; and as dirty a juvenile as one would wish to see; but he had about him all the airs and manners of a man. He was short of his age: with rather bow-legs, and little, sharp, ugly eyes. His hat was stuck on the top of his head so lightly, that it threatened to fall off every moment. . . . He wore a man's coat, which reached nearly to his heels. He had turned the cuffs back, half-way up his arm, to get his hands out of the sleeves. . . . He was, altogether, as roystering and swaggering a young gentleman as ever stood four feet six, or something less, in his bluchers. . . .

Said Fagin, 'My best hand was taken from me, yesterday morning. . . . He was charged with attempting to pick a pocket, and they found a silver snuff-box on him. . . . Ah! he was worth fifty boxes, and I'd give the price of as many to have him back. You should have known the Dodger, my dear; you should have known the Dodger.' . . .

'It's all up, Fagin,' said Charley. . . . 'They've found the gentleman as owns the box; two or three more's a coming to 'dentify him; and the Artful's booked for a passage out [is bound to be sentenced to transportation]. . . . To think of Jack Dawkins—lummy Jack—the Dodger—the Artful Dodger —going abroad for a common twopenny-halfpenny sneeze-box! I never thought he'd a done it under a gold watch, chain, and seals, at the lowest. Oh, why didn't he rob some rich old gentle-man of all his walables, and go out *as* a gentleman, and not like a common prig, without no honour nor glory!' . . .

'What do you talk about his having neither honour nor glory for?' exclaimed Fagin, darting an angry look at his pupil. 'Wasn't he always top-sawyer among you all! Is there one of you that could touch him or come near him on any scent? Eh? . . . What are you blubbering for?' ' 'Cause it isn't on the rec-ord, is it?' said Charley . . . ' 'cause it can't come out in the 'dictment; 'cause nobody will ever know half of what he was. How will he stand in the Newgate Calendar? P'raps not be there at all.' . . .

'Never mind, Charley,' said Fagin soothingly; 'it'll come out, it'll be sure to come out. They'll all know what a clever fellow he was; he'll show it himself, and not disgrace his old pals and teachers. Think how young he is, too! What a distinction, Charley, to be lagged at his time of life!' . . .

'What is this?' inquired one of the magistrates.

'A pick-pocketing case, your worship.' . . .

'Now then, where are the witnesses?' said the clerk.

'Ah! that's right,' added the Dodger. 'Where are they? I should like to see 'em.'

This wish was immediately gratified, for a policeman stepped forward who had seen the prisoner attempt the pocket of an unknown gentleman in a crowd, and indeed take a handkerchief therefrom, which, being a very old one, he deliberately put back again. . . . He took the Dodger into custody as soon as he could get near him, and the said Dodger, being searched, had upon his person a silver snuff-box, with the owner's name engraved upon the lid. This gentleman . . . being then and there present, swore that the snuff-box was his, and that he had missed it on the previous day, the moment he had disengaged himself from the crowd before referred to. He had also remarked a young gentleman in the throng, particularly active in making his way about, and that young gentleman was the prisoner before him. . . .

'Do you hear his worship ask if you've anything to say?' inquired the jailer, nudging the silent Dodger with his elbow.

'I beg your pardon,' said the Dodger, looking up with an air of abstraction. 'Did you redress yourself to me, my man?'

'I never see such an out-and-out young wagabond, your worship,' observed the officer with a grin. 'Do you mean to say anything, you young shaver?'

'No,' replied the Dodger, 'not here, for this ain't the shop for justice; besides which, my attorney is a-breakfasting this morning with the Wice President of the House of Commons; but I shall have something to say elsewhere, and so will he, and so will a wery numerous and 'spectable circle of acquaintance as'll make them beaks wish they'd never been born, or that they'd got their footmen to hang 'em up to their own hat-pegs, 'afore they let 'em come out this morning to try it on upon me. . . . Ah! (to the Bench) it's no use your looking frightened; I won't show you no mercy, not a ha'porth of it. *You'll* pay for this, my fine fellers. I wouldn't be you for something! I

wouldn't go free, now, if you was to fall down on your knees and
ask me.'

(c) On Planning a Burglary

'Now, my dear, about that crib at Chertsey; when is it to be
done, Bill, eh? When is it to be done? Such plate, my dear, such
plate!' said the Jew. . . .

'Not at all,' replied Sikes coldly.

'Not to be done at all!' echoed the Jew, leaning back in his
chair.

'No, not at all,' rejoined Sikes. 'At least it can't be a put-up
job, as we expected. . . . Toby Crackit has been hanging about
the place for a fortnight, and he can't get one of the servants
into a line.'

'Do you mean to tell me, Bill', said the Jew: softening as the
other grew heated: 'that neither of the two men in the house
can be got over?'

'Yes, I do mean to tell you so,' replied Sikes. 'The old lady
has had 'em these twenty year; and if you were to give 'em five
hundred pound, they wouldn't be in it.'

'But do you mean to say, my dear,' remonstrated the Jew,
'that the women can't be got over?'

'Not a bit of it,' replied Sikes.

'Not by flash Toby Crackit?' said the Jew incredulously.
'Think what women are, Bill.'

'No; not even by flash Toby Crackit,' replied Sikes. 'He says
he's worn sham whiskers, and a canary waistcoat, the whole
blessed time he's been loitering down there, and it's all of no
use.'

'He should have tried mustachios and a pair of military
trousers, my dear,' said the Jew.

'So he did,' rejoined Sikes, 'and they warn't of no more use
than the other plant.' . . .

'Fagin', said Sikes, abruptly breaking the stillness that prevailed; 'is it worth fifty shiners extra, if it's safely done from the
outside?'

'Yes,' said the Jew. . . .

'Then . . . let it come off as soon as you like. Toby and me were over the garden-wall the night afore last, sounding the panels of the door and shutters . . . there's one part we can crack, safe and softly.' . . .

'Is there no help wanted, but yours and Toby's?'

'None,' said Sikes. ' 'Cept a centre-bit and a boy. . . . I want a boy, and he mustn't be a big un. Lord!' said Mr. Sikes, reflectively, 'if I'd only got that young boy of Ned, the chimbley-sweeper's! He kept him small on purpose, and let him out by the job. But the father gets lagged; and then the Juvenile Delinquent Society comes, and takes the boy away from a trade where he was arning money, teaches him to read and write, and in time makes a 'prentice of him. And so they go on,' said Mr. Sikes, his wrath rising with the recollection of his wrongs, 'so they go on; and, if they'd got money enough (which it's a Providence they haven't), we shouldn't have half-a-dozen boys left in the whole trade, in a year or two.' Charles Dickens. *Oliver Twist* (1837–8): (a) Chapters VIII, XXVI; (b) Chapters VIII, XLIII; (c) Chapter XIX

(d) A Receiver and his Client

As he [Dicky Perrott] neared Weech's coffee-shop . . . there stood Weech himself at the door, grinning and nodding affably, and beckoning him. He was a pleasant man, this Mr. Aaron Weech, who sang hymns aloud in the back parlour, and hummed the tunes in the shop: a prosperous, white-aproned, whiskered, half-bald, smirking tradesman. . . .

'W'y, Dicky Perrott,' quoth Mr. Weech in a tone of genial surprise, 'I b'lieve you could drink a cup o' cawfy . . . an' eat a slice o' cake too, I'll be bound.' . . .

Mr. Weech with a gentle pressure on the shoulders, seated Dicky at the table. . . . He swallowed the last crumb, washed it down with the dregs of his cup, and looked sheepishly across at Mr. Weech.

'Goes down awright, don't it?' that benefactor remarked.

'Ah, I like to see you enjoyin' of yerself . . . you're the sort o' boy as can 'ave cawfy and cake w'enever you want it, you are. . . . That was a fine watch you found the other day. [Dicky had stolen a bishop's gold watch at a charity tea.] Y'ought to 'a' brought it to me. . . . You went and took it 'ome, like a little fool. Wot does yer father do? W'y 'e ups an' lathers you with 'is belt [Dicky's father, a thief himself, was urged to this course by his wife, who cherished her former respectability and hoped to bring Dicky up to be honest], an' 'e keeps the watch 'isself. . . . When you *find* anythink,' he said, 'jist like you found that watch, don't tell nobody, an' don't let nobody see it. Bring it 'ere quiet, when there ain't any p'liceman in the street, an' come right through to the back o' the shop. . . . An' then I'll give you somethink for it—money p'raps, or p'raps cake or wot not. . . . There's no end o' things to be found all over the place, an' a sharp boy like you can find 'em every day. If you don't find 'em, someone else will; there's plenty on 'em about on the look-out an' you got jist as much right as them. . . . Now, you just go an' find somethink,' he said. 'Look sharp about it, an' don't go an' git in trouble. The cawfy's a penny, an' the cake's a penny—ought prop'ly to be twopence, but say a penny this time. That's twopence you owe me, an' you better bring something an' pay it off quick. So go along.' . . . [Dicky 'finds' something as he is told.] Mr. Weech was busier now, for there were customers. But Dicky and his bulge he saw ere they were well over the threshold.

'Ah yus, Dicky,' he said, coming to meet him. 'I was expectin' you. Come in——

> *In the swe-e-et by an' by,*
> *We shall meet on that beautiful shaw-er!*

Come in 'ere.' And still humming his hymn, he led Dicky into the shop parlour.

Here Dicky produced the clock, which Mr. Weech surveyed with no great approval. 'You'll 'ave to try an' do better than this, you know,' he said. 'But any'ow 'ere it is, sich as it is. It about clears auf wot you owe, I reckon. Want some dinner?' ...

'Done?' queried Mr. Weech in his ear. 'Awright, don't 'ang about 'ere then. Bloater's a penny, bread a 'a'peny, cawfy a penny, cake a penny. You'll owe thrippence 'a'peny now.' ...

Dicky came moodily back from his dinner at Mr. Weech's, plunged in mystified computation: starting with a debt of two-pence, he had paid Mr. Weech an excellent clock—a luxurious article in Dicky's eyes—had eaten a bloater, and had emerged from the transaction owing threepence halfpenny. . . . As Mr. Weech put it, the adjustment of accounts would seem to be quite correct; but the broad fact that all had ended in increas-ing his debt by three halfpence, remained and perplexed him. . . .

[Dicky, slow to pay his debt, is accused by Weech of taking his 'finds' elsewhere.] 'Now don't you go an' add on a wicked lie to yer sinful ungratefulness, wotever you do,' he said severely. 'That's wuss, an' I alwis know. Doncher know the little 'ymn?——

An' 'im as does one fault at fust
An' lies to 'ide it, makes it two.

It's bad enough to be ungrateful to me as is bin so kind to you, an' it's wuss to break the fust commandment. If the bloater don't inflooence you, the 'oly 'ymn ought.' ... [Dicky, much to Weech's annoyance, is given the chance of an honest job, as errand-boy to an oil-man—who sold many of the goods stocked by a modern iron-monger. Weech calls on his employer in his absence.]

'I jist 'opped over to ask'—Grinder led the way into the shop —'to ask (so's to make things quite sure y'know, though no doubt it's all right) to ask if it's correct you're awfferin' brass roastin'-jacks at a shillin' each . . . seven-poun' jars o' jam an' pickles at sixpence . . . doormats at fourpence?' ...

'Cert'nly not!'

Mr. Weech's face fell into a blank perplexity. . . . 'Well I'm sure 'e *said* fourpence: an' sixpence for pickles, an' bring 'em round after the shop was shut.' . . .

Mr. Weech, with ingenuous reluctance, assured Mr. Grinder that Dicky Perrott had importuned him to buy the goods in question at the prices he had mentioned, together with others—readily named now that the oil-man swallowed so freely—and that they were to be delivered and paid for at night when Dicky left work. [The stratagem succeeds, and Dicky becomes a thief once more.] A. Morrison. *A Child of the Jago,* edited by P. J. Keating (1969), 70–1, 73, 77–8, 80, 99, 133–4

17 C. D. Brereton   Rural Crime

Most crime in the nineteenth century was urban in nature, though the countryside was not immune—for a discussion of the causation of poaching and rural crime in general, see extract 2. The description below comes from a book written to oppose the suggestion of the Royal Commission on a Constabulary Force that the rural areas needed protection beyond that provided by the parish constable, and thus the witness is biased. But his account of the crimes of a particular village (Great Massingham, Norfolk) probably gives a reliable picture of the quieter rural areas.

VILLAGE POPULATION, 850.

Corn stealing, Fowls, &c.

1826.—B—— and N—— were apprehended by the constable. These men had been notorious thieves and been watched by the constable for some time. On the night on which they were detected, he being suspicious that N—— would remove some stolen goods, watched him and took him alone in the dead of the night with corn in his possession.—B—— was also taken in his own house the same night. The prisoners were taken to the magistrates, committed, and sentenced at the quarter sessions to 7 year's transportation, from which they have not returned. Picklock keys and various articles of stolen property were found and identified. The constable had had these prisoners some time in view, and was considered to have acted with so much spirit, that a subscription of about £10 was raised for him in the parish and neighbourhood.

Sheep stealing.

1830.—S. B. was a suspected character, had been detected and brought to justice before by the constable on trivial charges. A sheep was stolen in the parish, the constable traced the footsteps the next morning to the house of the prisoner, where he found the mutton. The prisoner absconded, but the constable watched and took him on his return to his cottage in the dead of the night, kept him in hold till the morning, took him to the magistrates, and the prisoner was convicted on the evidence of the constable and transported for life.

Wood stealing.

1835.—H. N—— had been a bad character. Had been before detected by the constable and imprisoned. Was supposed to have been a common thief. Was detected in wood stealing and transported for 7 years.

Poaching.

1835.—James C—— was apprehended by the constable twice in one year in the act of poaching and convicted.

Sheep stealing.

1836.—Robert L—— and William B—— common labourers, were, on information given by a farmer of the loss of a sheep, detected by the constable. In this case one of the prisoners was traced by the constable a considerable distance to his house, where after a long search, a bloody shoe and afterwards a sheep-skin were found concealed. The constable knew that the other prisoner had been drinking with this man, and he therefore searched his garden, where he found the other prisoner's footstep, and a pit in which was some wool, which indicated that a sheep had been buried. The footsteps were traced and the carcase found in an adjoining field. Both prisoners were tried, convicted and transported for life. The evidence in this case as in the former, was collected by the constable who received the county allowance.

Housebreaking.

1836.—John R—— and Valentine G——. In this case the robbery was committed in the neighbouring parish, but the prisoners lived in the parish of this constable. A stable door was broken open and goods to the value of £9, stolen. Information was given to the constable the next morning, who immediately went in pursuit of the prisoners whom he immediately suspected to have committed the robbery. He pursued them to Lynn and found them there. Called in the constable of Lynn to assist him, apprehended the prisoners, found the stolen property part at a private house and part at a pawnbroker's. The prisoners were committed, tried at the sessions and transported for seven years. In this case the constable considers he was money out of pocket.

Fowl stealing.

1836.—James S——. In this case two ducks and two geese were stolen; information was given to the constable who immediately examined the premises and perceived a footstep which he recognized, and traced it to the house. The prisoner was absent, searched the house, and found the fowls. The prisoner was convicted and sentenced to six months, first offence.

Poaching.

1836.—John C—— apprehended by constable in the act, and convicted.

Riot.

1836.—The constable considers that this year, (the building of the Workhouse) was a year of great excitement and crime.

John N—— and William B——, for rioting on occasion of building the workhouse, at the meeting of the guardians. The prisoners were identified by the constable, who, with a warrant, apprehended N——. B—— resisted and escaped, but afterwards surrendered himself. The sentence, 12 months imprisonment.

Poaching.

1836.—John W——, chimney sweeper, and William B——, both detected in poaching by the constable, and convicted.

Corn stealing for horses.

1836.—R. F——, a farming servant, apprehended by the constable, who watched him in the night in the barn. The farmer forgave the prisoner and refused to prosecute.

1837.—No case of consequence.

Larceny.—Linen stealing.

1838.—G. H——. On information of the robbery, the constable suspected the party, went to his house, and on searching found a part of the linen. The prisoner was apprehended by the constable and committed, and convicted, 6 months and hard labour.

Egg stealing.

1838.—S. C—— and W. W——, the latter only convicted, the constable having assisted in obtaining the information.

1839.—W. C——. This was a case in an adjoining village. This constable was called in to examine into some trifling malicious acts, and found out in his search by night, stolen corn, of stealing which the prisoner was convicted and sentenced.

Donkey stealing.

1839.—W. W—— a migratory thief, birth and parentage not known. The donkey was stolen in a neighbouring town. The constable found him offering it for sale at an insufficient price. Immediately charged him with having stolen it, but the prisoner asserted it to be his father's. Apprehended him, and gave information in the neighbourhood, the owner was found, and the prisoner convicted at the quarter sessions. C. D. Brereton. *Refutation of the Constabulary Force Report* (?1839), 95–9

18 Olive Malvery   White Slaving in 1912

Olive Malvery (Mrs A. Mackirdy), an Anglo-Indian singer, was one of those who, towards the end of the nineteenth century, disguised themselves to gain first-hand experience of the ways of down-and-outs in London. (James Greenwood—see extract 36—was one of the first to do this, but the most famous was probably Jack London.) She published her experiences in *Soul Market*, 1906. She founded Shelters for Women and Girls in London, and later turned to more polemical literature, *The White Slave Market* of 1912. This extract comes from that book, and is from a factual account of white-slaving in the East End of London written by W. N. Willis (1860–1922), an Australian and former member of the New South Wales Parliament, who had actively assisted Olive Malvery in much of her work.

If there are any "doubting Thomases" as to the extent of this fearful trade, I would strongly recommend them to visit Leman Street Police Station, where—if they have proper authority to put questions—that clever officer, Chief-Inspector Wensley, will soon tell them of the awfulness of the situation and the crying urgency that exists for speedy remedies in the shape of Parliamentary enactments that would give the authorities a strong arm to speedily stop, and perhaps kill, the illicit trade of "traffic in white women."

Almost weekly, glaring cases of the traffic in young girls who are taken abroad come under the notice of the Leman Street police, but in nine cases out of ten the police are powerless. Now and again they do succeed in bringing home the terrible offence, but even when they do, the law deals mildly with the offender. It is, indeed, a fact that the "pimp" who breaks the heart, the health, and every hope on earth of a white girl and who lives on her awful earnings in London is, when caught— which is seldom—treated far more leniently than a women's franchise enthusiast who emphasises her Parliamentary inequality by breaking a window or two.

As recently as April 14th this year, one of the numerous gang who are living on the ill-earnings of unfortunate women was arraigned at Bow Street before Mr. Curtis Bennett. The "sister of the pavement" who gave information to the police, complaining of the man's conduct in taking her immoral earnings from her, was a good-looking young English girl about twenty-five years of age. She stated that she had known the accused "bludger" for about fifteen months, and during that period, with the exception of some six weeks, he had lived on the money she had earned on the streets. As a rule he never got out of bed till about midday, and he had a fearful aversion to work. Sometimes, when she had no money to give him, he beat her most unmercifully. The result was that she was black and blue. Finally she left him. After that he wrote her letters threatening to "kick her inside out" if she did not send him money. It was quite true that this wretch had given her diamond rings, but he had purchased them with money she had made on the streets. The woman told the magistrate that she had given this "bludger" as much as £12 within a week, and that he had only given her a few coppers when she went out in the evening to look for more money. The unfortunate woman declared that she stood in hourly terror of the man's brutality.

The magistrate asked if the accused were a foreigner, and Detective-Sergeant Broadhurst replied, "No, sir, I wish he were."

The magistrate: "So do I."

The brute received sentence of three months for living on the results of the woman's prostitution, and three months for beating her when she had no money to give him.

This is one of the cases where the "bludger" is caught and dealt with under the authority of the law; and, as the law now stands, this human monster is penalised in about half the sentence he would have received for breaking a plate-glass window if he had belonged to the suffragette league, or if he had not belonged to any league, but, simply as a matter of getting money easily, had stolen a policeman's watch, for which no British Court would have given him less than twelve months. But for living on the prostitution of an unfortunate woman—who is forced to sell her body to men and her mind to the devil—this "bludger" gets three months, and three months more for beating and kicking her when she has no money to give him.

A case is recorded at Leman Street against two oily-tongued wretches—young Jews, good-looking, well dressed, and apparently free with money—who decoyed two handsome girls, both Jewesses and, I am told, both well-behaved. These girls were trapped at Whitechapel and shipped off to that fearful burial-ground for thousands of our girls—Buenos Ayres. The police showed me the photographs of these girls. They were well developed and comely. I also saw the picture of the "pimps." One would take them to be anything but "pimps."

The method they adopted to decoy these girls is the old, old story: fine clothes, silk stockings, a castle to live in, and servants to fan you. However, there was a noise about the disappearance of these girls. The Leman Street police got on their track, and as sufficient evidence was forthcoming, a warrant was granted. Chief-Inspector Wensley had the matter in hand, and the men were arrested in Buenos Ayres, extradited back, and convicted. One, named Cohen, received twelve months; the other, named Gold, fifteen months. Probably both names were assumed. The girls were restored to their parents. These men were only two of the many traffickers in girl-flesh, and how many girls they took off to Buenos Ayres, before they were caught, Heaven only knows. O. Malvery. *The White Slave Market* (1912), 272–5

PART THREE

The Statistics of Crime

One basic problem confronting all who seek to think constructively about crime is that it is very difficult to determine, even approximately, the number of crimes committed in any given period or place. There is much modern literature on the subject (the problems are well set out in N. Walker. *Crimes, Courts, and Figures* [1971]), and in the nineteenth century people knew of the pitfalls too. Edwin Chadwick, for example, declared in 1829 that there was no evidence for the general belief that crime in London had been steadily increasing since before 1815; all that had happened, he felt, was that there were more prosecutions, thus exposing more crime to the public view. However, the men of the early nineteenth century, learning the rudiments of the science of statistics as of so much else, gave a considerable amount of attention to the statistics of crime, which figured prominently in the first dozen volumes of the *Journal of the Statistical Society of London* (founded in 1834). The Society's first two secretaries, R. W. Rawson and Joseph Fletcher, were active contributors on the subject, to which attention had been called by the work of the continental writers A. M. Guerry and A. Quetelet. Though subsequent generations did not display quite so much enthusiasm, discussions of criminal statistics—and criticisms of over-reliance upon them—can be found throughout the period.

19 The Criminal Statistics

Though there are scattered series of earlier date, the first

continuous series of criminal statistics for the whole of
England and Wales dates from 1835. From that year to 1856,
the *Criminal Statistics* published each year gathered together
figures about those tried on indictment in the higher courts.
From 1857 the enlarged series known as the *Judicial Statistics*
included information about those dealt with summarily in
the magistrates' courts as well. It included three sections.
The first part, known as the police statistics, gave, by police
districts, the numbers of persons and houses of known bad
character, the numbers of indictable offences known to the
police, and information about those arrested or proceeded
against summarily. The second part, the criminal statistics,
gave details by judicial districts of criminal proceedings, in-
dicating the numbers charged with various offences, the
result of the case and the disposition of those found guilty.
The third part, the prison statistics, gave details by county
and by gaol of those confined in prison, and also details of
committals to reformatory schools and industrial schools.
Each annual issue of the *Criminal Statistics* or the *Judicial
Statistics* had an analytical introduction, many of them—like
that from which the extract here is taken—written by
Samuel Redgrave (1802–76), the Home Office Statistician.

The completion of the Police system under the Stat. 19 & 20
Vict. c. 69. has afforded great facilities, not previously existing,
for ascertaining facts which bear directly upon the criminal,
vagrant, and suspected classes—for recording the crimes committed—and the numerous infractions of the law which are now
dealt with summarily by Justices. The Police Returns which are
abstracted for the information of Parliament pursuant to the
requirements of the above Statute, are evidence of the value of
the police labours to the statist and to all who would investigate
the state of crime and the conditions out of which crimes arise. . . .

An attempt was made last year by means of the police to
ascertain the number of thieves, prostitutes, and suspected persons of all classes at large in England, and for the first time their

Classes	1859.			1858.		
	Males.	Females.	Total.	Males.	Females.	Total.
Known Thieves and Depredators:						
Under 16 years of age – –	4,382	1,546	5,928	4,773	1,608	6,381
16 years and above – –	26,478	7,132	33,610	26,772	6,879	33,651
Receivers of Stolen Goods:						
Under 16 years of age – –	85	28	113	119	29	148
16 years and above – –	3,450	844	4,294	3,410	787	4,197
Prostitutes:						
Under 16 years of age – –	—	2,037	2,037	—	1,647	1,647
16 years and above – –	—	28,743	28,743	—	27,113	27,113
Suspected persons:						
Under 16 years of age – –	3,878	1,370	5,248	3,912	1,512	5,424
16 years and above – –	26,706	5,734	32,440	28,028	5,774	33,802
Vagrants and Tramps:						
Under 16 years of age – –	3,279	2,167	5,446	3,265	1,942	5,207
16 years and above – –	11,811	6,096	17,907	11,390	5,962	17,352
Total:						
Under 16 years of age – –	11,624	7,148	18,772	12,069	6,738	18,807
16 years and above – –	68,445	48,549	116,994	69,600	46,515	116,115

numbers were given as an ascertained fact, in opposition to the many estimates, chiefly of an exaggerated nature, which had from time to time been made. These calculations have been continued under the same definitions for the year 1859, and it is a strong corroboration of the accuracy of the information possessed by the police, that though very great differences appear on a comparison of the returns for the two years in the separate districts, as might be anticipated with regard to a body so largely migratory, yet the general total corresponds with peculiar exactness, as is shown by the following table (p 83.)

This table proves a general decrease of the males of every class, with the exception of the vagrants; and an increase of the female thieves, except those under 16 years of age: but with regard to the prostitutes an increase both of the juvenile and the adult, reaching together 7·0 per cent. The gross total it will be seen does not vary more than is represented by an increase of 0·7 per cent.

As the police districts differ so largely in the occupations, habits, and character of their populations, causing in some temptations and inducements to crime, contrasted with their almost entire absence in others, it will be of useful interest to continue the comparison made last year of some of those districts which represent most prominently these different classes of the population. In the following calculations the number of the criminal classes are shown and the proportion which they bear to the population of the census of 1851,—

	Criminal classes.	Prostitutes separately.
1. *The Metropolis.*—Including an average radius of 15 miles round Charing Cross, and comprising the District of the Metropolitan Police and the City of London Police	13,120, or 1 in 194·0	6,849, or 1 in 371
2. *Pleasure Towns.*—Brighton, Bath, Dover, Leamington, Gravesend, Scarborough, and Ramsgate	2,265, or 1 in 87·4	943, or 1 in 209
3. *Towns depending upon Agricultural Districts.*—Ipswich, Exeter, Reading, Shrewsbury, Lincoln, Winchester, Hereford, and Bridgwater	1,854, or 1 in 86·6	666, or 1 in 241

	Criminal classes.	Prostitutes separately.
4. *Commercial Ports.*—Liverpool, Bristol, New-castle-on-Tyne, Kingston-on-Hull, Sunderland, Southampton, Swansea, Yarmouth, Tynemouth, and South Shields –	9,389, or 1 in 96·4	5,221, or 1 in 173·4
5. *Seats of the Cotton and Linen Manufacture.*—Manchester, Preston, Salford, Bolton, Stockport, Oldham, Blackburn, Wigan, Staley-Bridge, and Ashton-under-Lyne –	6,090, or 1 in 124·6	1,616, or 1 in 469·7
6. *Seats of the Woollen and Worsted Manufacture.*—Leeds, Bradford, Halifax, Rochdale, Huddersfield, and Kidderminster –	2,779, or 1 in 137·0	681, or 1 in 559·2
7. *Seats of the small and mixed Textile Fabrics.*—Norwich, Nottingham, Derby, Macclesfield, Coventry, Newcastle-under-Lyne, and Congleton – – – – –	2,208, or 1 in 119·4	762, or 1 in 345·9
8. *Seats of the Hardware Manufacture.*—Birmingham, Sheffield, and Wolverhampton – – – – – –	7,685, or 1 in 54·4	922, or 1 in 453·5

So far therefore as population may be taken as the basis of calculation, the proportion of the criminal class is the highest in the three great centres of the hardware manufacture, 1 in 54·4, a very high proportion; and then at one jump follows a group of population of the most opposite class—the towns dependant upon the agricultural districts, 1 in 86·6; and the pleasure towns, 1 in 87·4; next the great commercial ports, 1 in 96·4; after these, with a marked diminishing proportion, follow the chief seats of the woven fabrics—the small mixed textile manufactures 1 in 119·4; the cotton and linen manufacture 1 in 124·6; the woollen and worsted manufacture 1 in 137·0; and lastly, contrary to many received opinions, the Metropolitan Districts, in a marked degree the least infested by the criminal classes, 1 in 194·0. These results have also the confirmation of the previous year's returns, from which the present only vary so far as to place the pleasure towns before instead of after the commercial ports, with which they have changed places in the rank of criminality.

The state of prostitution in the same town populations, so far as may be judged by the number of prostitutes harbouring within their limits, does not show any marked variation from the returns of the previous year. It will be assumed that the police would only include in this class, those who notoriously and obviously belong to it, and that there must exist on its limits a large number of immoral characters, not yet quite degraded to its level. Taking the foregoing groups of town population, the commercial ports stand first in bad notoriety, there the prostitutes amount to 1 in 173·4; next the pleasure towns, doubtless charged with the vices of other districts, 1 in 209·9; thirdly the small towns of the rural districts, 1 in 241·0. In the seats of the manufacture of the smaller textile fabrics, where the young of both sexes are closely brought together, 1 in 345·9; next in the metropolis, 1 in 371·6, followed by the seats of the hardware manufacture, 1 in 453·5, and lastly of the great cotton and linen manufacture, 1 in 469·7, and of the woollen manufacture, 1 in 559·2.

In the agricultural districts the bad characters would be more readily known and traced by the police than when hidden in the population of towns, and their relative number is high, especially if the prostitutes, who congregate chiefly in the towns, are omitted from the calculation. The total of the criminal class is,—

	Criminal classes.	Prostitutes separately.
9. *Eastern Counties:*—		
Essex, Norfolk, Suffolk, Lincoln– –	10,407, or 1 in 122·0	1,104, or 1 in 1150·2
10. *South and South-western Counties:*—		
Southampton, Wilts, Dorset, Somerset	9,644, or 1 in 106·7	1,394 or 1 in 738·7,
11. *Midland Counties:*—		
Cambridge, Bedford, Northampton, Hertford, Oxford, Bucks, Berks – –	8,966, or 1 in 102·5	639, or 1 in 1439·0

The police also returned the number and class of the houses of bad character in each district. They show on the total an increase of 4·6 per cent. upon the return of the preceding year, chiefly in the increased number of public houses and beer shops of bad resort, which may be due rather to the improved obser- vation of the police than to an actual increase of this class of houses. The total numbers were,—

Houses of Receivers of Stolen Goods	-	-	-				3,041
Houses the resort of Thieves and Prostitutes, viz.:							
Public Houses	-	-	-	-	-	2,811	
Beer Shops –	-	-	-	-	-	2,765	
Coffee Shops	-	-	-	-	-	428	
Other suspected Houses		-	-	-	-	1,946	
							7,950
Brothels and Houses of Ill-fame	-	-	-	-			7,991
Tramps' Lodging-houses	-	-	-	-	-		7,294
Total Houses of bad character			-	-	-		26,276

. . . The crimes known and recorded by the police are of the class which are proceeded against in the criminal courts to the exclusion of the lesser offences, and if it could be assumed that all such crimes are included in these returns, their numbers, when compared with the apprehensions which ensue, would be a successful proof of police vigilance. But though it may be concluded that crimes which from their atrocity or magnitude cause alarm and hue and cry will not fail to be known and recorded by the police, it cannot be supposed that the large amount of petty depredation which must result from the number of the criminal class already enumerated can be fairly represented by the 36,262 cases which appear in the returns under the wide definition of *Larceny*. Such a statement must rather be taken as a proof of how little accurate information is possessed of the extent of the pilfering and depredation which all the evidence in the returns tends to show must be successfully committed. . . .

On the apprehension of a person charged with any offence it is the first duty of the police to take him with the least delay before a magistrate, who determines whether there is sufficient evidence to warrant his being put upon his trial, and in that case commits him to the next sessions for trial, or, in default of such evidence, at once discharges him from custody, except in those cases, where a remand to prison is made for two or three days for further investigation. The following statement shows the exact terms under which the charges against the above persons apprehended were disposed of by the magistrates— 37·5 per cent. were at once liberated after a detention of probably only a few hours; 4·7 per cent. were discharged on finding bail to appear and take their trial; and 56·4 per cent. were committed to prison to await trial at the next sessions.

	Males.	Females.	TOTAL.
Discharged – – – –	6,887	3,291	10,178
Discharged on bail for further appearance if required – –	238	30	268
Bailed to appear for trial – –	1,048	241	1,289
Committed for want of sureties –	70	9	79
Committed for trial – – –	11,677	3,628	15,305
Total – – –	19,920	7,199	27,119

Very different results appear on an examination of the effect of the Police pursuit in the chief classes of the crimes committed. In the offences against the person, 2,579 crimes are recorded, out of which arose 2,768 apprehensions, more than one person being frequently implicated in such offences, and 1,908 commitments for trial, so that 73·9 per cent. of the cases were successfully pursued by the police, a very satisfactory proportion, making every allowance for the cases where more than one commitment ensues. In the violent offences against property, 4,433 crimes are followed by 2,204 apprehensions, and 1,609 commitments for trial, or 36·3 per cent., and probably of these two classes of crimes the great proportion are known to the police and included in these returns. Next follow the ordinary cases of theft, embezzlement, fraud, offences unaccompanied by violence; these, as I have already stated, appear very inadequately represented by the 41,370 cases reported. They moreover led to only 18,738 apprehensions and 11,437 commitments for trial, not more than 27·6 per cent. of the offences recorded, which confirms the opinion that up to this time there exists a great impunity and long career in petty thefts, when unaccompanied by such acts of violence as create alarm and stimulate prompt information to the police to be followed by active pursuit. . . .

In the year 1859 charges against the following large number of persons were determined summarily:—

	Males.	Females.	TOTAL.
Proceeded against – – –	310,690	82,120	392,810
Convicted – – –	213,494	44,316	257,810
Discharged – – –	97,196	37,804	135,000

30 April 1860
S. Redgrave. *PP*, LXIV (1860), 477, 479–83

20 F. G. P. Neison   Analysis of the Statistics

The criminal statistics were subjected to much analysis in the nineteenth century, like many other series in that age when statisticians were working out the rudiments of their science. F. G. P. Neison published his *Contributions to Vital Statistics* in 1845. In the third edition of 1857 he included a chapter on the criminal statistics, from which the extract comes.

From the age of 20 it will be found that in the male sex, crime, in each successive term of life given in the Tables, decreases at the rate of 33·333 per cent., and in the female sex, at the rate of 25 per cent.; so that if two Tables were formed, in one of which the numbers resulting from such a law were given, and in the other the actual number of criminals, the one Table, particularly in reference to the female sex, would be almost identical with the other. The following Abstract will shew the ratio of criminals according to the actual results for England and Wales during the years 1842–4, and also during the years 1845–8, as well as according to the theoretical law just alluded to; and in regard to the years 1842–4, it will be seen that in only one of the terms of the male sex is there any material difference between the two classes of results, while for the female sex, the

actual and the theoretical results are almost identical throughout the whole of the Table.

Proportion per cent. of Crime to the Population.

Age.	Males.				Females.			
	Actual Results. Tables I and XXII.		Law.		Actual Results. Tables II and XXIII.		Law.	
	1842–4.	1845–8.	1842–4.	1845–8.	1842–4.	1845–8.	1842–4.	1845–8.
20 to 25	·7702	·6702	·8536	·7290	·1459	·1506	·1452	·1497
25 ... 30	·5989	·5141	·5691	·4860	·1141	·1240	·1089	·1123
30 ... 40	·3794	·3240	·3794	·3240	·0817	·0842	·0817	·0842
40 ... 50	·2504	·2222	·2529	·2160	·0643	·0609	·0613	·0632
50 ... 60	·1694	·1334	·1686	·1440	·0466	·0385	·0460	·0474

... It must thus appear evident that whatever means may be
employed for the prevention of crime, or the treatment of
criminals, ought to shew their influence and bearing on the
male sex chiefly between the ages of 20 and 25. The following
Abstract ... will shew the relative tendency to crime in the two
sexes at the various terms of life (see table p 91).

It will be observed that in the male sex the tendency to crime
at ages 15–20 is somewhat less than in the next quinquennial
period of life; but a similar result does not appear for the
female sex during the period 1842–4, as the tendency to crime
at those two periods of life is nearly equal. F. G. P. Neison.
Contributions to Vital Statistics, 3rd ed (1857), 325–7

21 Departmental Committee on Criminal Statistics Report

When the enlarged series of *Judicial Statistics* had been run-
ning for nearly forty years, it was subjected to examination by
the Departmental Committee on Criminal Statistics. The
Committee's report, published in 1895, was severely critical
of the way in which many of the tables were compiled, and
doubtful of their value. (The Committee were not of course

| Age. | Ratio per cent. of Criminals to the Population, yearly. | | | | Number of the Population to which there is one crime yearly. | | | | Excess per cent. of Crime among Males. | |
| | Males. | | Females. | | Males. | | Females. | | | |
	1842-4.	1845-8.	1842-4.	1845-8.	1842-4.	1845-8.	1842-4.	1845-8.	1842-4.	1845-8.
Under 15	·0494	·0432	·0080	·0072	2024·7	2315·2	12500·0	13913·3	517·4	500·9
15...20	·6841	·6404	·1495	·1498	146·2	156·1	668·9	667·7	357·5	327·7
20...25	·7702	·6702	·1459	·1506	129·8	149·2	770·4	664·1	493·5	345·1
25...30	·5989	·5141	·1141	·1240	167·0	194·5	876·4	806·4	424·8	314·6
30...40	·3794	·3240	·0817	·0842	263·6	308·6	1224·0	1188·2	364·3	285·0
40...50	·2504	·2222	·0643	·0609	399·4	450·0	1555·2	1160·9	289·4	158·0
50...60	·1694	·1334	·0466	·0385	590·3	749·8	2145·9	2596·9	263·5	246·3
60 & upwards	·0813	·0688	·0186	·0157	1230·0	145·4	5373·5	6379·3	336·8	428·7

the first to have these doubts—throughout the century unofficial writers had challenged the value of statistics of crime.)
These extracts give an indication of the nature of the problems described by the Committee.

The first point to be determined in dealing with these Tables
is, what is to be included under the head "Offences determined Summarily." It clearly cannot include all summary
proceedings. There are many proceedings before courts of
summary jurisdiction which are purely civil, and could on no
supposition come within the scope of Criminal Statistics. On the
other hand, it is difficult to follow the ordinary technical distinction, treating as criminal only those cases where the proceedings commence by information, and result, if successful, in
a conviction, and excluding those which commence by com-
plaint and result in the making of an order.

There are various summary proceedings where the procedure
is not by information and conviction, but which approach
closely in character to those which are criminal, such as proceedings for sureties of the peace, where there is no conviction
and sometimes no actual offence proved, but which are in fact
often used for punitive purposes, and proceedings on affiliation
orders, &c., which by section 54 of the Summary Jurisdiction
Act, 1879, are enforceable as if the order were a conviction.
Should these be included among offences determined summarily?

On the other hand, there are many offences punishable
summarily which are not in their nature criminal: having a
chimney on fire, failing to secure a child's attendance at school,
disobedience to a borough byelaw or to road regulations under
the Highway Acts, are treated by English law as criminal
offences and punished on conviction by fine, which is enforced
by criminal imprisonment. Yet they can hardly be regarded as
really forming part of the crime of the country. Can they be
excluded from the criminal returns?

On investigation we found that on this point great diversity of practice had prevailed. No definite instructions had been issued, and each police force did as it thought best. Thus 145 police forces included orders to find sureties among summary convictions, most of them under the head "Breach of the Peace," some under the head "Common Assault," while 13 police forces excluded them altogether. 74 forces included and 92 excluded the making of affiliation orders. 116 included and 17 excluded orders under the Employers of Workmen Act, 1875. Orders for maintenance of relatives under the Poor Law Acts were included by 76 and excluded by 38. The several orders under the Public Health Acts were included and excluded in varying proportions. The making of an attendance order under the Elementary Education Act, 1876, was treated as a conviction by 121 police forces and excluded from the returns by 27, &c., and this alone brought under the head "Conviction" about 20,000 cases a year, where there was in fact no conviction. The orders on parents for maintenance of children in reformatory and industrial schools were included and excluded in about equal proportions.

It was clear that such variety of practice necessarily detracted to a very great degree from the value of former returns, and that it would be absolutely necessary to lay down some rule which should be uniformly adhered to in future.

After much consideration we arrived at the conclusion that the Table of Offences determined Summarily should follow strictly the technical definition of criminal proceedings, that is, should include all cases in which the proceedings lead up to a conviction, and should exclude all cases where the result is merely an order. We are satisfied that this is the only way in which a clear line can be drawn and accurate returns obtained from the police forces.

It is true that some cases not in their real nature criminal cases will thus be included, but we have found it to be impossible to draw any line which will exclude these and no others: they cannot be excluded, but they must be allowed for in all deductions drawn from the tables in which they are included.

The rule will, on the other hand, exclude certain cases of a *quasi-criminal* character, where there is no technical conviction. We considered it right that these should be excluded; but as they are interesting in themselves, and as they are sure to be returned by many police forces as convictions unless some other place is provided for them, we have decided to include these in a separate Table for *Quasi-Criminal* Proceedings. . . .

The chief defect in the old Police Tables, which were compiled from annual returns made by 191 separate and independent police forces, has been due to the absence of sufficient instructions to secure their preparation on a uniform basis. So far as we have ascertained the figures have been prepared by the police with great care and some degree of accuracy, but on many points they have been left without guidance, and have proceeded some on one principle and others on another. However great the care bestowed on the individual returns, if they are prepared by many persons working on different rules, the result of their compilation must necessarily be unsatisfactory. It would often have been better that they should all be wrong, provided they all made the same mistake, than that some should be right and others wrong.

The most striking instance of this is the diversity of practice, mentioned above, in the matter of what is to be considered as a summary conviction. Another will be mentioned presently in connection with the question of the mode of tabulating cases where one person is charged with several offences. . . .

We have, therefore, prepared a code of instructions for the police and have made it as full and as precise as possible. . . .

As, however, it is impossible to anticipate every difficulty, the police forces should refer to the Home Office on all doubtful points, and the more important decisions on these points should, as they occur, be introduced into the code of instructions. It is an essential function of a department entrusted with the collection of statistics to lay down and explain the rules for their preparation.

14. POLICE RETURNS.—TABLES OF CRIMES
AND APPREHENSIONS.

The returns of Proceedings in Courts of Summary Jurisdiction having been excluded from the Police Tables, the latter will comprehend only strictly police matters—returns of crimes committed, and of apprehensions, with figures showing the results of the apprehensions; returns of the character of persons prosecuted; and returns of the number of suspected persons at large, and of houses that are the resorts of criminals.

The Tables of Crimes Committed and of Apprehensions are among the most important in the volume, but they have hitherto been marred by serious defects which have been the subject of much criticism.

(1.) The most important defect has been the exclusion of cases of indictable offences tried summarily. Thus, under "Larceny" the column "Crimes Committed," included all cases of larceny where the thief was arrested and tried on indictment, and all cases where the thief was not discovered or not arrested, but it excluded cases where the thief was arrested and tried summarily. The result was that the proportion between crimes committed and apprehensions was entirely misrepresented. To take the figures for the year ended 29th September 1890, it would appear from Table 5 that, under the head larceny, there were 17,239 crimes committed and 4,386 apprehensions, giving 4 to 1 as the proportion of crimes to apprehensions, whereas on reference to Table 8 it will be found that there were 35,306 persons charged with larceny who were dealt with summarily. The figures should therefore be—crimes 52,545, persons apprehended 39,692, giving a proportion of about 4 to 3 instead of 4 to 1.

We propose, therefore, that the Table should now include *all* indictable offences, and we have introduced additional columns to show the numbers disposed of summarily.

(2.) Another defect was that from "Crimes Committed" all larcenies were excluded where the article stolen was under 5s.

in value, except cases where an apprehension actually took place. The object of this rule, which was established in 1867, was to secure uniformity in the returns, as some police forces had and some had not included larcenies under 1s. It is obvious that this rule detracted from the accuracy both of the number of "Crimes Committed" and of the proportion of apprehensions to crimes. . . .

We now come to three Tables (XXV to XXVII) which correspond to the Tables in the old Statistics entitled "Class of Persons proceeded against, &c." (Table 9), and "Number of known Depredators, Offenders, and Suspected Persons at large, &c., and of the Houses they frequent" (Table 2).

These Tables appeared to us among the least satisfactory in the volume, and we have had grave doubts as to the propriety of retaining them. The question of what constitutes a "Known Thief," a "Vagrant," a "Suspicious Character," had been left almost entirely to the discretion of the individual police forces, and on examination it became clear that they adopted widely diverse standards. Thus in the second of the two Tables it appeared that in 1890 there were in Liverpool 132 "known thieves" under the age of 16, in Birmingham only 23, in Bradford none, and in Manchester none. This extraordinary variation could be accounted for only by the fact of the police of the different towns taking totally different views as to what constituted a "known thief." Again, the total number of thieves and suspected persons in the county of Stafford, excluding the boroughs, was given as 2,806, a much larger number than in the Metropolis, where the figure was only 2,392. . . . We cannot state too clearly that these three Tables are not Tables which we should have ourselves proposed, and that we have only retained them because they have been given for many years. We consider them of no value whatever for comparisons between different police forces, and of little value for general comparisons between successive years, *PP*, CVIII (1895), 18–21, 23–4

PART FOUR

Policing

The nineteenth century inherited a policing system that was in part a medieval survival, though drastically overhauled and considerably augmented in the eighteenth century. The policing of London was by Peel's day undertaken by a complex network of institutions that had grown up through successive amendments to the medieval pattern. Four officers of medieval origin survived, mostly with changed form or function: the justice of the peace, the parish constable, the beadle and the watchman. (Country areas contented themselves with the first two.)

The JP of the early nineteenth century had a multiplicity of administrative functions not exercised by his modern descendant, but even in his duties in connection with crime he performed three tasks, whereas the modern JP performs only one. Like those of today, the justices of the early nineteenth century sat in court and also granted summonses and warrants; but in addition they were responsible (if anyone other than the victim was) for the detection and pursuit of offenders, and for the maintenance of law and order in general. In the former role they directed the activities of the detectives, where these specialists existed, or otherwise called on the parish constable to summon witnesses before them. In the latter sphere they had heavy responsibilities in time of riot (see L. Radzinowicz. *History of the English Criminal Law*, Vol IV, 106) and were charged with overseeing the routine urban patrol forces—the parochial night watches. Unpaid magistrates continued to handle the affairs of the provincial towns, but London had stipendiary magistrates in some number from 1792.

The parish constable was one of the unpaid, annually appointed officers of the parish, doing duty for a year as his turn came round. He was responsible for the execution of warrants, the preservation of order and for supervising the parish watch. Many people indeed preferred to pay a fine and be excused the duty of constable, or to hire a deputy, which is proof of the heavy burden of the post. In urban parishes there would be a number of constables for the year—four or five perhaps—each of whom acted as constable of the night in rotation. When on duty, they were required to attend the watch-house and to patrol the parish, and indeed many of them did so.

To assist the constable of the night, or to take his place if he neglected his duty, there was the beadle. In the metropolitan parishes of the early nineteenth century the beadle had become a minor salaried official, with daytime duties in connection with the Poor Law and night duty every few days (again there were often four or five beadles to a parish). Constable and beadle, or beadle alone, inspected the parish watchmen as they reported for duty in the evening and as they returned to the watch-house in the morning, and went round the parish, sometimes twice a night, to check that they were at their posts and awake.

The parish watches, though often criticised in the writing and pictures of the day, were not all inefficient. Medieval custom, codified in the Statute of Winchester of 1285, had placed on each householder the obligation to watch for a night as his turn came round, in person or by deputy, but by the nineteenth century local acts had in most metropolitan parishes replaced this obligation with the duty of paying a watch rate, from the proceeds of which a paid body of watchmen was maintained. It was at times alleged that parishes employed as watchmen those whom they would otherwise have had to relieve as paupers, but this was not always the case, and some of the parish watches of London were efficient bodies.

There were in addition to these parochial forces police officers
—salaried plain-clothes detectives attached to 'police offices'
(the magistrates' courts of London and one or two large provincial towns) and given the powers of a parish constable, though
over a wider area. They investigated offences where a reward
was promised or at least payment of their expenses could be
anticipated.

Finally, there were in London patrol forces superimposed on
the parish watches and giving extra protection. Under the control of the magistrates of the Bow Street Office there had developed the Horse Patrol to guard the roads approaching the
metropolis from highwaymen, the Foot Patrol in the centre of
the town, the Dismounted Horse Patrol between the two, and a
Day Patrol, again in the centre of the town.

This system was swept away in 1829, when the parishes
(other than those in the City of London) within 12 miles of
Charing Cross were united into one Metropolitan Police District
policed by one force. (The boundaries were extended and the
powers of the force increased in 1839.) The New Police, as
contemporaries called it, was extended to the boroughs as an
accidental consequence of the Municipal Corporations Act of
1835 (5 and 6 Will IV c 76). Section 76 of that Act required
borough councils to appoint a watch committee, which 'shall
appoint a sufficient number of fit men to be constables . . . by
night and by day'. In the larger towns at any rate this led to a
merger of the old night watch and the day police along the
lines developed in London. The problem of policing the counties was investigated by a Royal Commission in 1836–9 (13 and
14) but its recommendations for an extension of the Metropolitan Police were not accepted. Instead, the County Police
Act of 1839 (2 and 3 Vict, c 93) allowed the various quarter
sessions to form police forces for their county or part thereof if
they wished. In 1856, and in Scotland in 1857, legislation (19 and
20 Vict, c 69, and 20 and 21 Vict, c 72) required every county
to establish a police force, and a system of government grants
and government inspection was introduced. It gradually

brought all counties and boroughs up to an acceptable level of efficiency (see H. Parris. 'The Home Office and the Provincial Police in England and Wales, 1856–1870', *Public Law* [Autumn 1961], 230–55).

22 Select Committee on the Nightly Watch   Report

The Select Committee on the Nightly Watch of the Metropolis of 1812 was the first of a series of Parliamentary investigations into the topic. There had been earlier inquiries; select committees were appointed in 1772–4, and the subject was included in the Twenty-eighth Report from the Select Committee on Finance in 1798. However, the 1812 inquiry was the first of a new spate, which Professor Radzinowicz suggests is testimony to an increase in crime in London at the end of and after the Napoleonic Wars. The 1812 Committee was set up primarily as a result of the 'murders in the Ratcliffe Highway' in December 1811, when two families died in a brutal manner and much public alarm was occasioned— but it seems reasonable to infer also some anxiety about crime in general.

Another Select Committee on London's policing was set up in 1816 and continued to hear evidence and to make reports until 1818, and there were others in 1822 and 1828. Professor Radzinowicz points out that there were nine reports published on the subject of crime and its prevention in the years 1812 to 1828, as against four in the previous half-century. The series perhaps came to an end because the Committee of 1828 called for reforms in the policing system and gave Robert Peel his opportunity to establish the Metropolitan Police; the previous Committees had been content to recommend a continuance of the existing system, though they were conscious of some of its faults. The passage quoted from the 1812 report calls attention to the higher standard of policing in the City of London proper—the square mile which alone fell under the jurisdiction of the Lord Mayor and his fellows —and the laxer systems in vogue in the City of Westminster

—which had no central authorities worthy of the name and where the parishes or special boards of trustees were left to organise the night watch.

———

Your Committee have not failed to observe that the City of *London*, from the nature of its Magistracy, the description of its various public Officers, the gradation and subordination of their various classes, the division and subdivision of its local limits, affords an example of that unity, and of the dependence of parts on each other, without which no well constructed and efficient system of Police can ever be expected. If such a system could be successfully imitated in *Westminster* and its Liberties, and within the other adjacent Parishes which have hitherto formed an unconnected mass of scattered and uncontrouled local Authorities, considerable benefit might be expected to ensue; for Your Committee are disposed to concur in opinion with several of the witnesses, that a well arranged system of Superintendence, Vigilance, and Controul, would tend more to the prevention of crimes, by rendering it difficult to commit them, than any degree of activity in the pursuit and conviction of criminals after the crime has been committed: at all events, however, the two systems are not only not incompatible, but would necessarily afford mutual aid and assistance to each other.

This system of Watch and Ward, adapted by the Legislature to the City of London, is not a dead letter, but is kept alive and in action by the constant superintendence of the Marshals of the City, with their Assistants, who every night visit the different Wards and Precincts, and take care that the Constables, Beadles, and Watchmen of all descriptions, are alert and do their duty. Morning Reports are made to the Lord Mayor, as Chief Magistrate; deficiencies are noticed, as well as any disorders or irregularities, or other occurences of the night.

In ancient times, when the whole of the Metropolis consisted of little more than the City of London (properly so called) such a system might have been abundantly sufficient for its good government and security.

The City of *Westminster*, owing to its having never been incorporated, is not provided with the same means, and the same gradations of its public Officers, to ensure the unity and efficiency of its exertions for the prevention of crimes, by the same system of controul and superintendence.

But Your Committee have to observe, that by the Statute of the 27th of Elizabeth, presiding and subordinate Officers are appointed, and powers given to the Dean and Chapter, and to the High Steward and others, to make Regulations for the good government of the City of Westminster. . . .

The Statute of 14 George III C. 90, seems to have superseded this system. . . . It is a local Act applicable to the City and Liberties of Westminster, and certain other Parishes therein named; and, with great detail, prescribes the duties of Constables, Beadles, Patroles and Watchmen. . . . Other Parishes or Hamlets are governed by particular Acts of Parliament, authorising the raising of Rates for Watching and Lighting, and vesting powers in certain Commissioners or Vestries for carrying these purposes into effect; but in many cases, the execution of the Law is extremely defective, and in some cases the power of raising Money is inadequate; in others the full amount is not levied; the mode of watching generally bad, and the men employed, both in number and ability, wholly inefficient for the purpose.

In other Parishes there is no Legislative provision, and upon the whole, no uniform system prevails; and neither the Magistracy, or the Government, have at present any connection whatever with the state of the Watch, and no controul or superintendence over it. *PP*, II (1812), 2–3

_____

23 G. B. Mainwaring   The Present State of the Police
Parliamentary inquiries on the police were supplemented by unofficial criticism. George B. Mainwaring, a magistrate of Middlesex, was the son and partner of William Mainwaring, a banker who was Chairman of Middlesex Quarter Sessions from 1785 to 1816 and who introduced, say the Webbs, 'an

extensive system of corruption' (*History of Local Government*, Vol I, 562). George Mainwaring had to resign in 1822 from the lucrative office of Treasurer of Middlesex, after a public scandal. However, as Professor Radzinowicz remarks, he 'had an intimate knowledge of the working of the police system and no hesitation in exposing its defects'. In the passage here quoted he explains its strengths and weaknesses.

In the first place, a great addition must be made to the number of officers. . . . During the time in which I have acted in a public office, I have had within my jurisdiction two of the most extensive districts in the metropolis, one containing, according to the Census of 1811, a population of 160,000 persons; and that in which I am now placed, according to the same Census, above 300,000; in the former, there were six acting constables, and in the latter there have been, (till within a very short time past), the same number, two having been lately added, all differing necessarily in talent and fitness. Can, therefore, our present state be matter of surprise? Besides, this force, from the smallness of its number, is incapable of a right application; it is principally occupied in the apprehension of offenders, or wasted upon comparatively minor objects; in waiting or watching for the casual fees of ordinary warrant-serving, and in endeavouring to allay the angry passions, rather than to frustrate the criminal propensities of mankind; it has, in truth, almost exclusively an *ex post facto* operation. Under our present limited system it is the interest of officers to be concentrated at the office, remaining there, to take advantage of what *has* been done; instead of spreading themselves abroad, to prevent what *may* be done against society. Nor can it be expected to be otherwise; neither the pay nor the inducements of officers are sufficient to give the proper impulse to their exertions. They receive only one guinea per week as salary, all other legitimate emoluments being derivable from the public or from individuals requiring their assistance, *after* they have suffered either in person or property; consequently, the commission of crimes becomes the officers' pecuniary interest. There are not funds, and the magistrates have not the power to reward them for the performance of the more useful and arduous duty of prevention; the duty of prevention is constant; incessant vigilance can alone produce it; and it is absurd to expect it without the action of a sufficiently powerful stimulus. . . .

But, we have not yet seen all the mischiefs of which our present police may be productive: it is sufficiently melancholy to reflect that in principle, and in means, it is thus defective, and that the operation of our laws has frequently a tendency to augment rather than to diminish crime. But still further, however painful the continued examination of the system may be, we must not blind ourselves to the possible frightful contingency of its corrupting those who are engaged in its administration. I must unequivocally disclaim any imputation upon the persons to whom the foregoing observation refers; it is to the moral tendency of the system that I alone apply it.

Let us then examine the grounds of this apprehension as officers are now circumstanced; they may derive their emoluments in criminal cases from one or more of three sources: from the public, from the accuser, or the accused: from the public out of the county stock, by the order of the court, on alleged consideration for loss of time, trouble, and expenses whilst indictments and trials are pending. Large as the aggregate sum is, from which this supposed remuneration is given, it is on many occasions insufficient to cover the inevitable charges which are incurred, in waiting for days and sometimes for weeks successively, to attend parties to prefer an indictment or to appear at a trial. Officers are very frequently engaged as parties to several prosecutions in the same session; but the avowed principle of compensation to them is upon a computation of time according to the number of days which they have attended the court; in fact, paying them as for one prosecution, regardless of the exclusive attention which each case may have required for weeks or months before it could have reached a court of justice, and, perhaps justly grounding the order of the court upon the consideration that for such services they are rewarded as the servants of the police. The public allowance then affords little encouragement to the officers in the prosecution of offenders, and we have seen that it does not pretend to consider them in the prevention or discovery of offences.

Their next source of supposed reward, namely, from the accusers, if even it were an adequate inducement, is in its consequences highly exceptionable; police is for the protection of the whole public, for the poor as well as for the rich; but has not the present system of reward an inevitable tendency to make the rich rather than the poor, the objects of an officer's attention? The public, as we have seen, *do* not reward them, the poor, *cannot*; where then can a fair reward be expected, but in cases where the more wealthy require their aid? And are we to expect that this description of persons is of all others never to be actuated by interest? can this be right? and is it not possible that this species of reward may be directed more to restitution than punishment, and that officers may thereby be made instruments to defeat rather than to promote justice?

But we must not stop here; for after the review which we have just taken, may it not follow, that if officers be not properly rewarded, they may be corrupted? Most strictly confining myself to the principle upon which these observations are grounded, should I not further ask whether it may not, by possibility, be the officer's interest that the guilty should escape, rather than that the poor or the parsimonious should prosecute; always remembering that the wealthy and the generous are the only persons to whom *interest* would call his exertions. It is likewise impossible to exclude from our consideration the probable contingencies of an officer's life; his pursuit exposes him to the corruptions, and to a great degree, acquaints him with the corrupted part of mankind; he must therefore have need of a more than common virtue not to acquire a familiarity with the objects of his constant attention. It is in human nature that he should do so, and that his severity must thereby be relaxed towards those with whom, under our existing system of inadequate compensation, he is thrown into such dangerous contact.

Let us consider a few of the cases in which a misunderstood economy in the remuneration of officers may injuriously operate; first, in those where the preventive function, that of mere vigilance, is concerned; and secondly, in those where their actual authority begins in the apprehension of offenders, upon the commission of crime: in the former there may be an indirect, in the latter a direct, influence. . . .

Again, let us look at the more dexterous and daring class of depredators, who have talent as well as money to contrive and execute their plans. It is known that such persons will almost exclusively devote themselves for months to the perpetration of a great robbery; for instance, that of stage coaches and other conveyances carrying large sums of money; the plan of these persons being ultimately settled, a robbery of this sort is committed; may not here a prospective possibility of interest occur to the mind of an officer? for if any considerable part of the booty be undisposed of, will it not be the feeling and the interest of the sufferer, as well as that of all parties, that the affair be compromised, that the sufferer shall save a great part rather than lose the whole; that the robber should restore a part and escape conviction, and that the officer shall be doubly rewarded for the success of his common agency? Is it the interest of officers, under our present system, to destroy altogether these bold, and possibly profitable contributors to their gains? Various are the cases of greater or less influence, to show the *indirect* encouragement to crime to which I have adverted; but if our principle of police apply to one, it must be applicable to all. The immediate *direct* influence must be more frequent than the former.

Thieves, in their public haunts, are daily under the eyes of our officers; we know their manifold depredations, but how comparatively few are the apprehensions: and from the little pecuniary impulse to the proper discharge of an officer's duty, may not temptation here again seduce him to the breach of it?

if a valuable prize be the fruit of a successful and almost open robbery, is it impossible that interest may suggest a similar negociation to that which I have recently described, and the abandonment and participation of the property, upon the same principle of appropriation? Be it observed, that this is general reasoning; but shall a reasoning be rejected in the application to one part of mankind, which is applied to all other parts? When we know our corrupt and corruptible nature; when experience and daily observation show us the charms with which bribery assails and subdues the heart of man, should we not at least guard that class of men who are, of all others the most exposed to it? and are we doing so? But it may be said, Can this be prevented? If the question be put in the abstract, whether any mode of encouragement or reward can be devised which shall, in its universal operation, make it the officer's interest to trust to the bounty of the public, rather than that of the criminal, in every *possible* case and contingency; the answer must obviously be, that such a plan cannot be devised. This, however, is not the right question, nor is it the correct view of the subject. It is true that neither the Legislature nor the Government can put into the officer's pocket so much as a successful plunderer may in an EXTRAORDINARY case; but the Legislature and the Government may invite to the police, men of the best intelligence in the middling class of society, of unimpeached and unimpeachable integrity; they may, by giving to these persons adequate regular pay, by keeping alive in them a constant expectation of reward as the consequence of a vigilant and successful preventive service, and extending this expectation to the hour of disaster, infirmity, or superannuation, so raise the character, occupations, and objects of an officer's life, as to make it his *better lasting* interest to trust to the steady permanent provision of a liberal public, than to the casual and perilous participation of guilty acquisition. . . .

The constables annually sworn into office are, doubtless, subject to the call of public duty, and to the direction of the high constable when called; but the nominal list of constables does not constitute an effective establishment for the daily and nightly superintendence of the town; and, in several parishes, not a fifth part of those sworn in, take the routine duty of their office. Respectable tradesmen cannot, without detriment to themselves and a sacrifice of comfort, be so engaged; and the consequence is, that the parochial police must be left almost exclusively to those who make it a business and profitable pursuit...

In the review of our several means of protection, there is another very extensive establishment, namely that of the *nightly watch*, which may be urged as an argument against the necessity of resorting to the increase which I have recommended. This establishment has now acquired a prescriptive usage; it has identified itself with the feelings, and almost with the prejudices of our citizens; it gives an imaginary comfort if not real protection to thousands; and many would hardly lie down in their beds in peace, without knowing that these their guardians are abroad, and in the dead of the night are moving to proclaim the hour, to say that all is well, and that they may rest in security. Even these considerations must plead most powerfully against the dissolution of this establishment; but at present, though it may incidentally aid the minor objects, it cannot be available for the main purposes of police.

It must have occurred to the most unobserving passenger in our streets, and have been strikingly apparent to our police magistrates, that the vigilance of watchmen contributes little to the diminution of the higher class of offenders; it is to broils and affrays, and the sallies of intemperance, to which their services are principally called. Very large sums of money are annually expended upon this description of duty, the whole of which, even when it reaches a higher class of offenders, has entirely an *ex post facto* operation. A man who walks a given space of ground, and that at intervals, can only come in contact with those who pass whilst he is upon it; and will the lurking and secretly-contriving felon or burglar execute, or attempt to execute his purpose, when he knows that the watch is in the way, and will be soon out of the way? will he not so contrive his means as to effect his object unseen? In such case the watch, therefore, facilitates rather than frustrates his purpose. Besides, the known prescribed course of a watchman's duty, his lantern, his paraphernalia, and his half-hourly cries, are positive signals against approach: he is a common crier who, in fact by his presence, denotes his succeeding evanescence, and he acts as a moving light-house to warn off all advances till it disappear, which becomes the notice that all is clear and every thing safe. That this is a real and no figurative description, must be obvious to the most common understanding. There is besides in the watchman's life that which must prevent his being an effective police officer; up by night, to do his duty properly, he should be in bed by day; he cannot therefore, have the opportunity of becoming to any degree acquainted with the bad characters upon the town (a knowing indispensable to an effective officer). From the confined limits within which he acts, he acquires a sluggishness of movement, and torpor of character, and is deprived of that ubiquity of action which gives opportunity of watching or of pursuing the felon or the fugitive. But, it may be said, there is a watchman every where; granted that it is so, but can every succeeding watch know the *preceding* movements of the criminal; a knowledge, perhaps, indispensable to frustrate his ulterior purpose: so that, in fact, upon every fresh ground the criminal is a new man, and so on, through every succeeding space that he reaches. Such cannot be the case with a police of *unseen* and unconfined action. It must also be obvious, that the dull monotony of a watchman's occupation is extremely adverse to the right composition of their body. It has ever been, till of late years, the *pis aller* of society; and since the days of Shakespeare, has preserved the same characteristic features. From the laudable efforts of some parishes, a beneficial change has taken place in the appointment of these officers; but I am still persuaded that the institution has within it those inherent defects which must always be exposed more or less to the objections which I have stated as a means of *preventive* police. G. B. Mainwaring. *The Present State of the Police* (1821), 541–51

24 John Townsend   The Bow Street Runners

John Townsend (?1759–1832) was one of the most famous
Bow Street Runners, and became one of the two runners
detailed to protect the Royal Court. He was regularly engaged to appear at the Bank of England on Dividend Day,
and fashionable people would place on their invitations the
words 'Mr Townsend will attend', hiring him to protect
their guests from pickpockets. The nine pages of Townsend's
evidence to the Select Committee on Police of 1816 make
fascinating reading. As the garrulous old man rambles from
point to point, at times almost disregarding the questions put
to him, he builds up a picture of the work of the police officer
(the proper name for those generally called the Bow Street
Runners), not failing, as the extract shows, to mention the
faults of the system.

7th June, 1816

You are one of the Police officers at Bow Street?—Yes.

How long have you held that situation?—I think somewhere
about four-and-thirty years; rather better. . . .

*What, in general, do you consider is the nature and extent of the duties
of your office?*—The duty of the office, as a matter of course, is to
attend at the Office, and at other public things for the officers;
but two of us have been more immediately placed about the
Court. . . . When the Regent goes to Brighton, for instance,
Sayers and I go. There are two officers appointed at Windsor,
who are unconnected with the Office, Rivett and Dowsett . . .

. . . The usual way in distributing the £40 on conviction is,
that the Recorder gives the prosecutor from five to fifteen and
twenty pounds, according to circumstances, and the appre-
henders the remainder, that comes to, perhaps, only three or
four pounds a-piece, though the world runs away with the
ridiculous idea that the officers have £40. It is a singular circumstance, but in all cases of felony there are but two cases
where there is any reward at all; those are a highway robbery
and a burglary; all the others are mere bagatelles, for they are

merely certificates, what the vulgar call Tyburn-tickets, to free from parish-offices. . . . I have sold them as low as £12. In such a parish as St George's, Hanover Square, the people are of so much consequence that they will serve themselves. The highest is in Covent Garden, where it is worth £25; for the constable of the parish must sit up, I think, one night out of three; and whoever is hit upon as a parochial constable says, 'This is a hard thing, and therefore I will buy myself off;' and a ticket in that parish, therefore, is worth more. . . .

At how much should you estimate the ordinary profit which an officer of the Police makes from what is called the £40 Parliamentary reward? — . . . I have very great doubt whether there is an officer on the establishment who has ever made £30 a year by rewards. There are eight sessions in a year; taking it for granted that the officer should convict two felons for a burglary, or a highway robbery, each session, which I am certain they do not, because in many cases the Jury will take off the burglary, and the officer is left in the lurch; therefore it is a robbery, not burglariously breaking and entering, but stealing only; then the officers apply to the Judge for what they term their expenses, which they are allowed, which is somewhere about four shillings a day for their time; therefore I am perfectly satisfied they cannot get £30 a year. . . .

Should you not think it would be a much better mode of rewarding the services of the officers of the Police, if it was left in the breast of the Police Magistrates to pay, for every special service that each officer did, the reward which those Magistrates thought fit to apportion? — I have always thought so; from the earliest part of my time I have thought it, and for the best of all reasons; I have, with every attention that man could bestow, watched the conduct of various persons who have given evidence against their fellow-creatures for life or death, not only at the Old Bailey, but on the Circuits, and I have been perfectly convinced that would be the best mode that possibly could be adopted to pay officers, particularly because they are dangerous creatures; they have it frequently in their power (no question about it) to turn that scale, when the beam is level, on the other side; I mean against the poor wretched man at the bar: why? this thing called nature says profit is in the scale; and, melancholy to relate, but I cannot help feeling perfectly satisfied, that frequently that has been the means of convicting many and many a man; and I told Sir Charles Bunbury my opinion upon that subject 30 years ago, when he wanted to get rid of rewards, it should be in the breast of the Judges . . . whether they have convicted or not convicted the party, if they see the officer has done his duty towards the Public, and his duty fairly and uprightly towards all parties, they should have a discriminating power to pay that officer according to the nature of the case: then the officer does not stand up and look at this unfortunate creature, and swear to this or that thing, or the other thing, for what? for the lucre—for nature is nature, do with us what you will; and therefore I am convinced, that whenever A is giving evidence against B he should stand perfectly uninterested. . . .

Having stated the different objections to the officers of the Police receiving rewards, do you not think there is another objection also, namely, where the officers hold in their hands the balance of life and death in any evidence that they may give, it is possible that a rich criminal may have an influence over a needy officer highly injurious to the public interest?—No question about it; I will give the Committee a case in point. . . . Mr Ives, the gaoler in Surrey, before the trial came to me, and said, 'Townsend, you know Mother Usher very well,' 'yes,' said I, 'these ten years;' he said, 'Cannot these be stached?' meaning put an end to: I said no, it was impossible that it could be; because the case was very plain, and of all women upon earth she ought to be convicted. . . . I then lived in the Strand; two of her relations called upon me, trying to see what could be done, and they would have given me £200 not to have appeared against that woman. She was a very rich woman, and made over all her property before she was convicted; she got the best part of it by plunder. . . . How is it possible to avoid those temptations, provided the officer so employed has not the means of barring off those temptations by being paid liberally for what he does; for however we may be, in whatsoever state we are placed, nothing can be so dangerous as a public officer, where he is liable to be tempted; for, God knows, nature is at all times frail, and money is a very tempting thing; and you see frequently, that much higher characters than Police officers and thief-takers, as they are called, have slipped on one side, and kicked over places; . . . I, it is true, have steered clear, but I do not owe that to any merit myself. I have been lucky enough to have situations where I have been very very liberally paid . . . but I have a fellow-feeling for other officers, and I must say, that I think that some of the officers deserve every praise, . . . and I cannot help again repeating, that nothing but their industry would enable them to get through the piece; for what is so small a stipend as a guinea a week? *PP*, V (1816), 137–141

25 James Grant   The New Police

The New Police—the Metropolitan Police, which first went out on the streets of London on 29 September 1829—had their opponents, many of them vehement in their rejection of 'Peel's bloody gang'. Much of the agitation died down, however, when central funds assumed 2d of the 8d rate demanded of the parishes, and within a few years the force had won complete acceptance, at any rate from middle-class articulate opinion. The extract comes from the work of James Grant (1802–79), editor of the *Morning Advertiser* 1850–71, and a prolific writer about life in London and elsewhere.

When the new police were formed in 1829, the total number was 3314. These consisted of 17 superintendants, 68 inspectors, 323 sergeants, and 2906 constables. Since then, the number has been gradually increasing. What it is at present, I have not been able to learn; but six months since it was, in round numbers, 3500. These 3500 are entrusted with the protection of the persons and property of about a million and a half of her Majesty's subjects; that being supposed to be the amount of the metropolitan population, exclusive of the City. If this estimate of the population of London outside the walls of the City be correct, it would give us one police constable to every 425 persons.

The new police are under the control of two commissioners, each having a salary of 800*l.* per year. The present commissioners are Colonel Rowan and Mr. Richard Mayne. The 17 superintendants have each an annual salary of 200*l.* The 68 inspectors severally receive a yearly salary of 100*l.*; the 323 sergeants individually receive 58*l.* per annum for their services; while the pay of the common constables is 19*s.* per week. Where the party is single, a deduction of one shilling is made in the event of lodgings being found for him. If married, and lodgings are found for the party, a special agreement must be made in each case. In addition to his weekly pay of 19*s.*, the private constable is entitled to as much clothing as is equal to two suits in the course of a year. The entire yearly expense of the metropolitan police is 240,000*l.* Of this sum, 60,000*l.* is paid out of the consolidated fund, and the rest is made up by a rate on the parishioners.

The district embraced by the metropolitan police is formed into seventeen divisions. . . . It is also stipulated in the "Instructions" given, that the men belonging to each section shall, as far as may be found practicable, lodge together near to the place of their duty, in order to render them speedily available in case the services of such as are off duty should be required for any special emergency . . . The letter of the alphabet marked on the collar of each policeman's coat, denotes the particular district in which he serves. A represents Whitehall; B, Westminster; C, St. James's; D, Marylebone; E, Holborn; F, Covent Garden; G, Finsbury; H, Whitechapel; K, Stepney; L, Lambeth; M, Southwark; N, Islington; P, Camberwell; R, Greenwich; S, Hampstead; T, Kensington; and V, Wandsworth.

The course to be adopted when a person wishes to become a member of the metropolitan police force, is sufficiently easy and simple. He has only to present a petition to the commissioners, accompanied with a certificate as to good character from two respectable householders in the parish in which he resides. Inquiry is then made relative to the parties signing the certificate; and it being found that they are respectable men, whose testimony as to the applicant's character may be relied on, his name is put on the list of eligible candidates for the situation whenever a vacancy shall occur. I need scarcely say that, before appointment, the party is examined by a surgeon, to see that he suffers under no physical defect which would prevent the efficient discharge of his duties. It is also requisite that he should be under thirty-five years of age, and that he be five feet eight inches in height. The average time which an applicant has to wait, after his name has been inserted in the list of persons eligible to the office, is about eight weeks. Should, however, a party deem it an object to get appointed with the utmost practicable expedition, he may succeed in the short space of ten or twelve days, by getting some personal friend of either of the commissioners to use his influence on the applicant's behalf. The usual form of a petition and certificates from rate-payers, and so forth, are dispensed with in such cases. All that is necessary on the part of the applicant is, that he be able-bodied, the proper height, and not beyond his thirty-fifth year.

Nothing could be more complete than the organization of the metropolitan police. Each party or company is divided into fours; the first four being on duty for a given time, and the other four coming to their relief, just as in the case of soldiers, whenever their allotted period has expired. It is the duty of the sergeant to see that this arrangement is strictly attended to, and also that the parties take the night and day watches alternately. Two of the inspectors are always on duty at once. One of them examines into the state of matters throughout the division; for which purpose he is constantly going about among the men: the other inspector is stationed at the watchhouse to receive charges, complaints, and all applications for assistance. The various sergeants throughout the division regularly report to the inspectors the existing state of affairs within their respective districts. When the men are relieved, they must all assemble at a particular spot, just as when about to go on duty, in order that the sergeant may see that they are all sober, and as correctly dressed as when he marched them to the scene of their duties. It is thus impossible that any dereliction of duty or improper conduct can take place in the case of any of the men, without its being immediately brought under the notice of the superintendant; and through him, where the case may be such as to require it, under the notice of the commissioners. The latter gentlemen may dismiss any of their men at a moment's notice, and without assigning any reason for such dismissal. It is from time to time impressed on the mind of each police constable, that he must make himself perfectly acquainted with all the parts of the streets, courts, thoroughfares, outhouses, &c., of the section of the metropolis constituting his beat. He is also expected—a thing which may at first sight appear impossible— "to possess such a knowledge of the inhabitants of each house as will enable him to recognise their persons." He is further expected to see every part of his beat once in ten, or at least fifteen minutes, unless in such cases as it may be deemed necessary to remain in a particular place for a longer period, to watch the conduct of some suspected person. A printed copy of instructions as to how he shall act in almost every conceivable case, is given to the police constable on his appointment to the office. . . .

It is to be regretted, for their own sakes, and indirectly for the sake of the public, that no provision, in the shape of pension, is made for those of the new police who may be disabled from the performance of their duties while engaged in the public service, or when old age overtakes them. . . . What a miserable prospect for these men do advanced years present! By the time they attain a certain age, they will, in the nature of things, be unfit for the continued discharge of the duties of their office; and just at that moment they will be turned adrift without a farthing in the world and without the physical ability to earn as much as would procure them the most scanty means of subsistence. . . . Were their pay such as that with prudence and economy they might contrive to make some provision for old age, the matter would be different; but it is barely sufficient, in such a place as London, to afford them the means of a homely subsistence. No man, not prepared to deny himself the most common necessaries of life, could save a sixpence out of nineteen shillings per week. . . .

The new police were for some time very unpopular. There was a natural tendency in the minds of the people to look with suspicion on a body with very enlarged powers, and which had been constituted in a manner different from any previous constabulary force which had been known in this country. These suspicions were converted into positive apprehensions by the clamorous opposition got up to the new police by one or two journals circulating largely among the lower orders of the community. Every movement they made was narrowly watched; and every action they performed was made the subject of severe criticism—often of downright misrepresentation. . . . The vast diminution, however, in the amount of crime committed in town, and the great addition to the number of cases in which the offenders were detected, taken into custody, and prosecuted to conviction, soon became sufficiently apparent to remove gradually the prejudices so strongly and generally entertained against the new force, and to make it popular with the public. The experience of nine years has confirmed the predictions of good from it, made by the authors of the measure. Person and property are now incomparably safer than they were under the old system. The new police are now the objects of universal approbation, and most deservedly so. . . .

The integrity and trustworthiness of the new police, considered as a body, are above all praise. It is surprising in how few instances charges of corruption have been preferred, far less proved, against any of their number. One scarcely ever hears of such a charge. There seems to be a spirit of rivalry as to who shall be the most honest—if the expression be a proper one—as well as to who shall be the most active and enterprising among the body. . . .

I have said that there has been a great diminution in the amount of crime committed in London, since the institution of the new police. Almost all the extensive confederations which then existed for the purpose of carrying on a regularly organized system of robbery, and other crimes against property and person, have been broken up, and scattered in all directions. We no longer hear of acts of wholesale plunder, or of thieves being leagued together, and carrying on an organized system of war against property, in bands of twenties or thirties. What is now done, in the way of housebreaking or felony, is usually done by some adventurer on his own account, or by small partnerships of two or three. Nor do we now hear of the ingenuity of former thieves, in defeating the ends of justice; an ingenuity which often gave an air of rich romance to the adventures of the parties. The thieves of the present day, owing to the vigilance of the new police, have but few and slender opportunities of displaying any ingenuity they possess; in other words, their "affairs" are not now attempted on that large and daring scale on which they were formerly done. Ingenuity itself finds it impossible to get even skilful plans of robbery laid, far less executed. The achievements of our present thieves are poor and spiritless, compared with the triumphs of their predecessors ten or twelve years since. J. Grant. *Sketches in London* (1838), 387–92, 397

___

26 Policing in the 1850s

By the middle of the century the New Police had spread to about half the counties and most of the larger boroughs of England and Wales. In 1853 a Select Committee 'to consider the Expediency of adopting a more Uniform System of Police in England and Wales, and in Scotland' was appointed. The faults arising from an incomplete adoption of the new system are described in the passage below, taken from the evidence to the Committee. Captain William Charles Harris, the witness here quoted, was Chief Constable of Hampshire from 1842 to 1856, and then Assistant Commissioner of Police for the Metropolis until his retirement in

1881. He was (after Admiral John B. B. M'Hardy, 1801–82, Chief Constable of Essex, 1840–81) a pioneer of the new model of county policing, and was a leading expert witness for the Select Committee.

26th May, 1853

Captain *William Charles Harris*, called in; and Examined.

1. *Chairman*.] YOU command the constabulary in Hampshire?—I do.

2. For how many years have you done so?—For 10 years. . . .

7. . . . I have a return of the counties in which the Act has been adopted; it has been adopted for the whole of 22 counties in England and Wales, in parts of seven others; but in 22 counties the old parochial system still continues.

[*The Witness delivered in the following Return:*]

RETURN of the several Counties that have adopted the Provisions of the Constabulary Act

For the whole County:

Bedford.	Salop.
Cambridge.	Southampton.
Durham.	Stafford.
Essex.	Suffolk.
Gloster.	Surrey.
Hertford.	Wilts.
Lancaster.	Worcester.
Leicester.	Cardigan.
Norfolk.	Carmarthen.
Northampton.	Denbigh.
Nottingham.	Montgomery.

In Parts only:

Cumberland.	Warwick.
Dorset.	Westmoreland.
Rutland.	York.
Sussex.	

10. Can you generally say that the adoption of the police

under the Act has proved efficacious in Hampshire?—In my opinion it has; serious offences are rare, and in most cases followed by detection; petty depredations are prevented, vagrancy checked, and beerhouses controlled.

11. Can you refer to any documents to prove that crime has decreased in Hampshire since the police force has been established?—Yes, by reference to the criminal returns of the force under my command (1851), it will be seen that since the year 1847, the year in which a register of offences was first commenced in Hampshire, the offences against property, as likewise the value of property lost, and the crime undetected, have all gradually decreased. . . . (See table p 121.)

23. Mr. *Fitzroy*.] What principal boroughs are there in Hampshire?—There are several boroughs in Hampshire; but Portsmouth and Southampton are the most important.

24. *Chairman*.] You would call them first-class boroughs?—Yes; there are likewise the boroughs of Winchester, Andover, Newport, Basingstoke, Romsey, and Lymington.

25. In which of those boroughs has the police force been consolidated with the county police?—Andover for some years, and Lymington recently.

26. Sir *J. Trollope*.] Can you separate the payment for those boroughs which have been consolidated with the county?—In the case both of Andover and Lymington there is merely an arrangement made by which 65 *l.* per man is paid to the county, which is the average cost of the whole of the constables. . . .

30. *Chairman*.] Do you think the expense of the constabulary in the county and boroughs together, would be materially increased by the union of the boroughs with the county?—No; if the whole were consolidated into one force the expense to each would be lessened. . . .

34. Mr. *Rich*.] You have stated that you think it would be conducive to an efficient police, if the police of the boroughs were incorporated in the police of the county; will you state the inconveniences which now result from those boroughs not being

SUMMARY of the Number of FELONIES affecting Property that have been Committed during the undermentioned Years, within the Jurisdiction of the *Hants* Constabulary; showing the First Amount of Loss, and the Amount Recovered, the Number of Persons Committed for Trial, and the Number of Undetected Offences.

Year.	Number of Felonies.	AMOUNT OF LOSS.			Number of Persons Committed for Trial.	Number of Offences Undetected.	Per-Centage of Undetected Crime on the Number of Offences Committed.
		First Loss.	Amount Recovered.	Total Loss.			
		£. s. d.	£. s. d.	£. s. d.			
1847	709	1,880 5 3	541 11 11	1,338 13 4	334	388	54
1848	687	*3,405 9 9	†523 19 1	*2,933 10 8	374	329	47
1849	678	869 1 −¼	316 − 8½	553 − 4	369	348	51
1850	615	777 13 5¼	261 19 3¼	515 14 2	350	290	47
1851	609	723 9 10	246 14 8¼	476 15 1½	316	281	46

* 2,141 *l.* of this amount was timber stolen from the New Forest.
† 52 *l.* of this amount was stolen in Berkshire.

incorporated?—The want of co-operation between boroughs and counties is a great evil; if the forces were consolidated fewer men would be needed. The boroughs are generally the central points from whence criminals issue into the surrounding districts to commit offences, and to which they return with their plunder; the town force having no interest in the prevention or detection of offences committed in the county, parties are allowed to pass unquestioned.

35. Mr. *Fitzroy*.] Can you tell the Committee in which of the boroughs in Hampshire there is a police force separate from the county?—Portsmouth, Southampton, Winchester, Newport, and Basingstoke.

36. Mr. *Rich*.] You say you find there is a want of co-operation in the police force?—Yes, there is a want of co-operation; there is no denying that a jealousy exists between the two forces, but not in my opinion to such an extent on the part of the county as the boroughs, the county constabulary being the larger force of the two. Our men are always willing to afford assistance to the borough police. I will mention a case of the want of co-operation which recently occurred: one of the superintendents of the Hants constabulary was proceeding on duty from the Southampton terminus in plain clothes, when he saw in the train a desperate character, who a year and a half previously had effected his escape by violence from two of the constables of our force; the superintendent immediately seized him, and brought him out of the train; the superintendent sent to the borough station to borrow a pair of handcuffs to secure his prisoner; the loan of these was refused; "they had none to spare;" and the only mode of securing the prisoner was by his leaving him in charge of the railway officials, and proceeding into the town to call upon one of the borough police to aid and assist in the Queen's name, and thus he obtained the handcuffs.

37. Are your superintendents in communication with the superintendents of the borough police?—Not in constant communication.

38. In the event of the occurrence of a crime, do your superintendents immediately communicate the fact of that crime having been committed to the superintendents of the various boroughs?—Certainly they do, if it is a matter of importance; they would not perhaps mention a petty depredation.

39. Inversely, do the superintendents of the boroughs communicate with your superintendents?—Very rarely. . . .

64. Sir *J. Trollope*.] You would save some of the higher classes of appointments if you consolidated the boroughs with the county, you would save having a higher class of officers over each separate borough as at present?—You would be obliged to have a police superintendent at Portsmouth and at Southampton.

65. How many superintendents have you?—Fourteen.

66. What is your next grade?—Sergeants.

67. How many sergeants have you?—Fifteen; I should say that there is one chief clerk who ranks as a superintendent.

68. He is entirely confined to office work?—Exclusively. . . .

71. Supposing some of your men are taken to another county with prisoners for trial, and have to attend to give evidence against them, are they allowed to make out a bill *ad libitum*?—I stop their pay whilst they are absent on the duties of another county, and they receive their allowances as ordinary witnesses.

72. How are those allowances regulated?—In the county to which they go, for mileage and attendance; I stop their pay as long as they are in the service of another county.

73. What is your stoppage per head, per man, for the superannuation fund?—Two and a half per cent.

74. Mr. *Fitzroy*.] After how many years are the men entitled to superannuation?—Not till they are 60 years of age.

75. What is the amount of the police force now in Southampton?—I am speaking from recollection; but I think it is 28 or 30. Not more than 30.

76. Is that an efficient force?—I should imagine not. The subject of an increase of 10 men to the force was only brought before the Council last week. . . .

78. You said that you would shift the constabulary?—Yes.

79. Do you attach much importance to that?—Very great importance. I would not allow a constable to remain for a day after it had come to my knowledge that he was locally connected. If it was reported to me that a police constable had got into low company, I should shift him immediately.

79.* In bringing those other boroughs, which are now independent of you, under your authority, you would be able to exercise the same power of shifting the constables in these boroughs?—Yes.

80. Do you consider that mischief arises to the boroughs from the constables not being shifted?—Yes; it is impossible that a man can do his duty if he is locally connected. If police constables become acquainted with beershop keepers, for instance, it is impossible they can do their duty. If I see any indication of intimacy of that kind, I remove the constable to another part of the county, perhaps 40 or 50 miles away. . . .

91. Mr. *Phillips*.] I think you said you shifted the constables from Andover in order to avoid the evil of local connexion?—Yes.

92. Do not you think you incur in some degree the risk of want of local knowledge from such a practice?—No.

93. Sir *J. Trollope*.] You do not move them all at once, I presume?—No, we only move one man at a time; we seldom move a superintendent.

94. Have you any difficulty in finding residences for the men? —Where the county has not built or provided stations, the men take private lodgings.

95. Has the county of Hampshire built any stations for the accommodation of the police?—Yes.

96. What number?—Several divisional stations have been built; in divisions where there is no station the property of the county, stations are rented.

97. Where there are stations with buildings attached to them, have the constables lodgings found by the county?— They pay for them.

98. Then when there is a change of men there is always a residence for them?—Where there is a station built.

99. Are those men provided for in other houses?—The men provide their own lodgings, and pay generally about 2s. a week.

100. Mr. *Fitzroy*.] What do the men pay to the county for lodgings?—The same amount.

101. What is their weekly pay?—Our constables are in four classes, at 15s., 17s., 19s., and a guinea a week.

102. Sir *J. Trollope*.] If the county do not find the lodgings, do they hire them, and stop the cost out of the pay of the men? —No.

103. What is the system which is adopted?—The men find their own lodgings; but if there is a county building, then we stop the amount from their pay at the rate of 2s. a week; I see the amount stopped for lodgings last year was 126 l. 6s. 3d. . . .

116. Mr. *Fitzroy*.] What is the average area which each of your constables have to watch and superintend?—The area of the county, including the boroughs of Andover and Lymington is 1,006,210 acres, and we have 176 men to that acreage. . . .

209. Mr. *Rich*.] Is the police force popular in the county?— Very; at least I do not know anything to the contrary; we have no petitions for a decrease of the force, but we have many petitions presented to the court of quarter sessions for an increase.

210. Is the feeling of the masses of the people favourable or unfavourable towards the police?—I know nothing to the contrary of the feeling being favourable.

211. Have you had any remonstrances from the ratepayers as to the expense?—I cannot call to mind having heard of any.

212. You stated that you would recommend that the constables should be drilled to the use of arms?—Yes.

213. Do you consider that that would be an additional means for the preservation of the peace of the county?—I consider that it would not only tend to the preservation of the peace of the county, but it would form a great element of national de-

fence, if the men were drilled to the use of arms. The men are young, energetic, and active, and patrolling for seven hours every night of their lives, are in splendid condition for marching.

214. Do you think that it would tend to make the force itself more popular, and that the men would feel additional self respect?—I think it would myself.

215. Do you think that there would be any germ of unpopularity in the idea of constables being armed?—I do not indeed.

216. You are not afraid that accustoming them to the use of arms would raise a feeling of jealousy on the part of the population of the county?—No.

217. *Chairman*.] Do you contemplate using them as a military body for police purposes?—I merely suggest that the men should be drilled to the use of arms, but not carry them except on the occasion of a threatened invasion, or when some serious disturbance of the public peace has taken place, or is apprehended, when an Order in Council might be given.

218. You mean that they should be armed only on such occasions as a military force would be employed?—Yes.

219. Mr. *Rich*.] For the suppression of riots, for instance?—Yes.

220. Sir *J. Trollope*.] Are the constables allowed any cutlasses?—The whole body is drilled to the use of the sword.

221. Is the night patrol armed?—Some few constables are supplied with cutlasses, whose beats are so situated, that in the opinion of two justices of the county it is necessary for their personal protection in the performance of their duty.

222. Are they armed when they assist the coast guard?—No.

223. *Chairman*.] Do they never carry arms except under an order from two magistrates?—Except on any sudden emergency, when I have issued orders for the men to be armed; when I report the same, and the reasons for such order, to the Secretary of State, and any two justices of the peace, as soon afterwards as is practicable.

224. Mr. *Fitzroy*.] Are the constables drilled to the use of the cutlass?—Yes, to the use of the sword.

225. Mr. *Rich*.] Are many of the constables old soldiers?—No; I have an objection to old soldiers.

226. You prefer young men?—I do not like to take men who have been soldiers, even after three or four years' service; they are invariably addicted to drinking. . . .

27th May, 1853
Captain *William Charles Harris*, called in;
and further Examined.

674. *Chairman*.] I THINK you stated, after your examination yesterday, that you wished to add something to your evidence, as to the efficiency of the county constabulary over the superintending constables, in following in pursuit of criminals?—I wish merely to mention one case which occurred in Hampshire, illustrating the advantages of a county constabulary over that of superintending constables. A poor man's house in the parish of Sherfield English was broken into during the absence of the family at church; the circumstance was reported to the superintendent of the Romsey division, who proceeded at daylight the next morning to examine the premises; and having found the tracks of several individuals, he made inquiries, and ascertained that four men and two women had been in the neighbourhood the day before. From inquiries, he was led to believe that they had taken the Salisbury road, and he tracked them through Whiteparish and Whaddon into Salisbury. From further inquiries he found that a party answering the description had slept in Salisbury the night previous, and were gone on the road to Wilton. Beyond Wilton he overtook the party, and, pulling up his horse, he waited until they came to a wall, when he drove alongside of them, and turning his horse's head sharp into the wall, directed the constable who was with him to jump out before, whilst he got out behind, thus enclosing the party between the cart and the wall. The party showed fight, but he knocked two of them down, and throwing their sticks over the

wall, he handcuffed the four men, and made them and the women get into his cart, and thus conveyed the whole back to Salisbury. All the stolen property was found in the possession of the persons apprehended. I merely mention this fact to show that whether a poor or a rich man is robbed, the county constabulary proceed at once to do their duty; whereas a superintending constable would have to stop to inquire who was to pay him his expenses. So it is with the borough police; they have no means of recovering their expenses if they are unsuccessful in pursuit; and thus many a zealous officer, who is anxious to discharge his duty, is deterred, by risk of losing his money, unless the prosecutor or person robbed is sufficiently wealthy to guarantee him his expenses.

675. You mean that the difficulty in following in pursuit in this case was from its being a poor man's house that had been robbed?—Yes; in the case I speak of, the man would not have been able to furnish the superintending or parish constable with the means of following in pursuit. *PP*, XXXVI (1852-3), 5-8, 11-14, 21, 49-50.

---

27 Housing the Police

The following letters illustrate one of the problems of policing the heart of the metropolis in the middle of the nineteenth century. The housing shortage was regarded as a crime-producing factor, as we have seen (5), but it had its problems for the police also. The Commissioner of Police of the City of London (Daniel Whittle Harvey, 1786–1863) was reluctant to allow his men to live outside the City, in case he needed to gather them together at a moment's notice in the event of riot; his alternative solution of building quarters for them was, however, only partially implemented, and his successor had to agree to his men's requests in 1877. (See D. Rumbelow's excellent study of the City Police, *I Spy Blue*, 1971.)

Memorial of the Police Force.

Sir,

We, the undersigned inspectors, sergeants, and constables of the City of London Police Force, beg most respectfully to solicit your kind intercession in our behalf, that we may be relieved from the great difficulties we now have in obtaining lodgings (particularly we who have families), from the unhealthiness of the places we are compelled to reside in, and from the enormous rents we are obliged to pay.

The difficulties we experience have gradually increased for some years, and are likely to continue in consequence of the alterations and improvements made for railways, new streets, and buildings. A great number of houses in the city formerly tenanted by families have been pulled down, and warehouses and offices erected upon their sites. Porters and others of that class are more numerous, and the demand for lodgings has increased, while the supply has been and continues to be so seriously diminished.

The houses we are compelled to reside in are situated in densely populated and unhealthy courts, each room in the house being generally occupied by a separate family. In such crowded houses we are continually disturbed, and frequently do not get a sufficient amount of rest.

The majority of us can afford to occupy only two rooms, and more than eighty members of the Force with their families, each numbering from one to four children, many of them over ten years of age, are living in one room, and paying, in many instances, for that room, 4s. per week. Being obliged to wash and to dry our clothing, to live and to sleep nightly and daily in a single room, it is never thoroughly ventilated, and our health is in consequence very seriously impaired.

We not only have occasion to feel degraded and ashamed of our places of residence, but we are often subjected to annoyance through living in the same house with persons of disreputable character, with whom our duty brings us in frequent contact;

E

and in changing a residence, many fruitless hours are spent daily, and even weeks consecutively, in procuring another.

We beg to submit to your consideration that, if the restriction compelling us to reside within the city should be withdrawn, we could get small convenient houses at the same rent we are now paying for one or two rooms.

We should experience the comforts and advantages of a well-regulated home; we could bring up our families to have a due regard for decency, our health would be much improved, and we should be able to obtain that rest and quiet which is indispensably necessary to the proper discharge of our duties.

The abundant proofs you have given us of your earnest desire at all times to promote our welfare, induces us to hope we may, in this matter, receive your highly valuable support.

We have the honour to be, Sir,

Your most obedient humble Servants,

[Here follow the signatures of 13 inspectors, 67 sergeants, and 390 constables, who weekly pay for lodgings an average, for one room, 3s. 7d.; two rooms, 4s. 8½d.; three rooms, 6s. 5d.; four rooms, 7s. 9d.]

To Daniel Whittle Harvey, Esq.
Commissioner City of London Police Force.

Report of the Superintendent of the City Police.

24th January, 1861.

Sir,

In obedience to your order, I submit in writing my opinion upon the effect to be anticipated in the event of permission being granted to the married men of the Force to reside out of the city.

In the first place, if granted indiscriminately to all our married men, comprising nearly five-sixths of the Force, we should at once lose all control and supervision over them while off duty.

Secondly, as frequent occasions arise for the attendance at the stations of constables off duty, to answer inquiries or give particulars of matters which have occurred within their knowledge, great inconvenience and loss of time would result from the necessity of taking men from their beats to bring those constables from distant residences.

Again, as it is an invariable and necessary rule that every man on the sick list should be visited constantly and at uncertain intervals at his residence, in order to prevent imposition, and to ascertain whether he is doing all in his power for the restoration of his health, the absence of the sergeants from their districts on these distant visits would seriously interfere with their sectional duties.

Further, as it is required of every sergeant to certify that he has tested the correctness of the addresses given in monthly by the constables under his charge, he must for considerable intervals of time leave those on duty on his section unchecked by his supervision.

Another useful rule of the Force would be rendered impracticable: it is now required of those on night duty that they call sufficiently early every constable living on their beats who is upon the morning relief, by which means alone can we ensure the punctual attendance of large numbers of men at so early an hour as a quarter to six. This advantage would be entirely lost, as we could not use the metropolitan constables in charge of the beats upon which our men would be residing for such a purpose.

Lastly, the important means we now possess of collecting, upon emergencies, at any given place, all men off duty, by passing a verbal order to their residences through those on duty on the beats, would be no longer available.

For these reasons, I respectfully submit that the residence without the city of any considerable number of its constables would be seriously detrimental to the efficiency of the Force, and must greatly diminish the control which it is so essential to maintain over its individual members.

Although, for the causes above stated, I cannot conscientiously recommend compliance with the application of the married men to reside out of the city, yet I feel the full force of their representations in respect to the daily increasing difficulty of finding decent accommodation for themselves and families within their very limited means.

I respectfully, however, submit that all the grievances of which they complain can be remedied, and their health and comfort promoted, without having recourse to any such objectionable expedient as that they propose. The suggestion made by yourself to the Committee, a few weeks since, that a building for the accommodation of the married men should be erected at each end of the city, upon the principle of the model lodging-houses for families, would effectually meet the requirements of the Force . . . not only would our men obtain all the advantages of cheap residence, with good ventilation, water, gas, washing and drying conveniences, and a large central area as a play-ground for their children, but the Force would acquire a never-failing reserve of men to meet serious emergencies.

I have the honour to be, Sir,
Your obedient faithful Servant,
(Signed)   CHARLES G. HODGSON,
Superintendent.

Daniel Whittle Harvey, Esq.
   Commissioner of the City Police.
    W. Dent. *Observations on the Displacement of the Poor* . . . (1861), 30–33

PART FIVE

Punishment

Methods of punishment were much discussed in the nineteenth century. The first reform was to remove the accretion of statutes carrying the death penalty; it is often said that at the beginning of the nineteenth century there were over 200 capital offences, though the exact number is probably impossible to compute. The laws were often not enforced—indeed, as extract 28 shows, this was a prime plank in the reformers' platform—for the possibility of the criminal suffering the final penalty was generally considered to deter prosecutors and jurors rather than criminals. By 1837 the work of reform had mainly been done in this field.

The task of finding satisfactory forms of non-capital punishment was, of course, more difficult (after all, it remains unsolved). The prison system of the nineteenth century was twofold until 1878. There were the national prisons holding the convicts, those sentenced to death or transportation or, later in the century, to penal servitude, and the local prisons for other sentences of imprisonment. The former were under the control of the Secretary of State for the Home Department, the latter of the local justices in quarter sessions.

The hulks, part of the national system, began to be used in 1776 as a temporary expedient, because convicts could no longer be sent to the American Colonies; they persisted, however, until 1858, when at last sufficient land prisons were provided. Transportation to Australia began with the First Fleet, which arrived there in 1788. The fate of a convict in Australia might be very good or very bad (see 31b, and Marcus Clarke's *For the Term of His Natural Life*, 1870, for a dramatic but accurate picture of the worst side of the transportation system), and the impact of transportation was much discussed until its abolition, at the insistence of the Australians, in the 1850s.

The regimes for prisoners confined in land prisons in this country passed through a number of stages. In the early part of the century the unclassified prisons had still many of the faults that John Howard had criticised. Acts of 1823, 1824 and 1835 (4 Geo IV, c 64; 5 Geo IV, c 84; and 5 & 6 Will IV, c 38) had done much to improve matters. However, the requirements of classification led to a forty-year debate between supporters of the separate and the silent systems. These two attempts to prevent contamination of the relatively innocent by the truly guilty originated in America. The separate system demanded that a prisoner should come into contact only with prison staff, and because each man had a cell to himself it was often called, and no doubt often was, solitary confinement—though in principle the prisoner was to have frequent contact with other people. The silent system aimed at avoiding the expense of the separate system by rigidly enforcing silence between prisoners.

The Prison Inspectors created by the act of 1835 favoured the separate system, and from 1865 this had to be adopted in all prisons. In 1878 both local and national prisons were placed under the care of the Prison Commission, a body responsible to the Home Secretary. Under the first chairman, Sir Edmund Du Cane (1830–1903), the Prison Commissioners set out to provide a regime of 'hard labour, hard bed and hard fare', and British prisons became soul-destroying institutions. In 1895 the Gladstone Committee—the Departmental Committee on Prisons (37)—re-emphasised the idea of reformation, and the long movement away from the Du Cane model to our own began.

The treatment of juveniles was early recognised as a special problem. There was a special hulk for juveniles (30) and Parkhurst Penitentiary was established in 1838. Youngsters were

often given favourable treatment—'We contrive to bend the
laws', said one magistrate—and in extract 38 one judge describes his own unofficial efforts at reformation. Institutional
treatment for juveniles took a new direction in the middle
1850s, when reformatory schools and industrial schools were
established on an increasing scale. The former received those
who had committed crimes punishable with imprisonment,
whereas the latter took children who had committed less
serious offences or lived in such circumstances that they seemed
in imminent danger of becoming criminals. The reformatory
schools received legislative sanction in 1854 (17 and 18 Vict, c
86), and the industrial schools in 1857 (20 and 21 Vict, c 48).
From the late 1850s opinion was virtually unanimous concern-
ing the beneficial effects of the new schools (39a and b are
typical).

Finally, the Borstal system was introduced in 1902 for
prisoners aged sixteen to twenty-one. In the prison at Borstal,
near Rochester, a new system of treatment was devised, and it
was successful enough to be adopted elsewhere and to give its
name to a new class of institution (40).

28 House of Lords   Capital Punishment

The reform of the laws relating to capital punishment
spanned the years 1808–37 (by which latter date capital
punishment was in practice almost entirely reserved for *For murder*
murder). The following extract from a debate in the House
of Lords in 1820 portrays well the tone of the discussions
throughout the period—the careful rationality of the reformers, alert to stress the limited extent to which the harsh
laws were applied, and the gloomy foreboding of their
opponents, meeting humanity with humanity but worrying
about the dangers about to be unleashed about the heads of
the people.

The third Marquess of Lansdowne (1780–1863) was
Chancellor of the Exchequer at the age of twenty-five in the
'All-the-Talents' ministry of 1806–7, and inherited the title in

1809. Thereafter he was one of the acknowledged leaders of the Whig Party and was Home Secretary 1827–8, and Lord President of the Council in the periods 1830–41 and 1846–52.

Lord Eldon (1751–1838) was Solicitor-General from 1788 and Attorney-General from 1793 until 1799, and in the latter capacity was active in the repressive legislation of the period. In 1799 he became Lord Chief Justice of the Common Pleas, and in 1801 Lord Chancellor, holding the office until 1827 (with a brief break in 1806–7). He became a by-word for delay and resistance to reform: by 1855 Walter Bagehot could write of him, 'As for Lord Eldon, it is the most difficult thing in the world to believe that there ever was such a man. He believed in everything that it is impossible to believe in,— in the danger of Parliamentary reform, in the danger of Catholic emancipation, in the danger of altering the Court of Chancery, in the danger of abolishing capital punishment for trivial thefts, in the danger of making landowners pay their debts'.

House of Lords 17 July 1820

The Marquis of *Lansdown*, on moving the order of the day for the third reading of the Privately Stealing bill, said, that there were three bills before the House . . . for the amendment of the criminal laws of the country. . . . They were now to consider the propriety of repealing a bill which had remained for a considerable time a dead letter on the Statute Book, and which, instead of assisting, prejudiced the course of justice, by deterring prosecutors from taking that part which they ought in order to bring criminals to account. Owing to its severity, it had hardly been executed during the last 60 or 70 years. . . . In the greater number of cases, the prosecutors preferred acquiesing in the loss of their property, rather than expose their consciences to the feeling of having visited on their fellow-creatures a disproportionate, cruel, and unjust punishment. He found by the returns, that from 1805 to 1818, 352 convictions had taken place, and only one execution. In London and Middlesex there had been but one execution during a whole century. . . .

The Lord Chancellor [Eldon] said, . . . while it appeared a harsh thing to condemn a man to death for stealing privately in a shop to the amount of five shillings, the present bill did not provide sufficiently against the loss of property to an amount which, though it could not distress some, might effectually ruin many shop-keepers. The act was not intended merely for the protection of men of large property, but also of men of small property, who could not so well protect themselves. . . . If hereafter it should be found, that shop-lifting became universal, and that many persons were reduced to misery by this crime, he hoped it would be remembered that he had suggested the consideration, whether this law which had so long existed was not wise and politic. . . . On the third reading he should propose an amendment to provide that persons stealing to the value of more than 10l. should still be subject to the capital punishment. . . .

As to the repeal of the 6th Geo. 2nd, which affixed the punishment of death to persons breaking down the banks of rivers or sea-banks, when he looked to the state of property in Lincolnshire, where, by offences of this kind, mischief might be done, to which the robbery of a few pounds was not to be compared—when persons might be deprived of all their means of subsistence, he could not give his consent to it. . . . He next came to the clause respecting threatening letters, which took away the capital punishment unless the letter demanded money or a valuable consideration. On this he confessed he had great doubts. Nothing was more destructive to the peace of families, than the apprehensions which were kept alive by the malicious and secret threats of mischief. Hansard, *Parliamentary Debates*, New series, Vol II, cols 491–3, 496

---

29 L. O. Pike Corporal Punishment

Corporal punishment—whipping and flogging—was used throughout the nineteenth century. Whipping was by common law a punishment for misdemeanour, and when the general provision of the death penalty for felony was removed in 1827 (7 & 8 Geo IV, c 28), it was provided that, if no other punishment was specified by statute, a male felon could be 'once, twice or thrice publicly or privately whipped' in addition to imprisonment. Some of the statutes that provided penalties for particular felonies also made provision for whipping. Justices had lost their power to order whipping for minor offences by the Vagrancy Act of 1824 (5 Geo IV, c 83), but the Juvenile Offenders Act of 1847 (10 and 11 Vict, c 82) empowered courts of summary jurisdiction to order juvenile offenders under the age of fourteen to be whipped; in 1850 the age limit was raised to sixteen (13 and 14 Vict, c 37).

The Criminal Law Consolidation Acts of 1861 (24 & 25 Vict, cc 96–100) removed the powers the courts possessed to whip persons over the age of sixteen (with trifling exceptions) but the flogging of adults was re-introduced for garrotting and robbery with violence during the outbreaks of the former offence in 1862–3, by the Security from Violence Act, 1863 (26 & 27 Vict, c 44). In 1912 the Criminal Law Amendment Act (2 & 3 Geo V, c 20) extended this punishment to procurers or males living on immoral earnings. These variations in the power of the courts to order floggings for adults did not affect those already sentenced and confined in prison, and flogging could be and was used as a means of prison discipline throughout the century. (The law as stated in these paragraphs relates to England and Wales, and the situation in Scotland was often different.)

L. O. Pike, author of a historical study of crime published in 1873–6, was one of those who doubted whether the introduction of flogging had much to do with the cessation of garrotting, and he did not support the demand, current at the time he was writing, for a further extension of corporal punishment to meet an outbreak of brutal assaults. The detailed description of a flogging that he included in his history may perhaps have been intended as ammunition for those who opposed corporal punishment.

As now inflicted, the punishment of flogging can have but little moral effect save upon the person who endures it and the person who actually administers it. Few or none are present *Description of* except the officials of the gaol or visiting justices; *the present* spectators are not admitted within the prison *mode of flog-* walls to see a fellow human being beaten when *ging: the ob-* they have no better motive than mere curiosity. *jections to it.* The prisoner is fastened to a 'triangle,' or to an apparatus somewhat resembling the stocks, so that he can move neither hand nor foot. His back is bare. The man who wields the cat shakes out its nine thongs, raises it aloft with both hands, and deals the criminal the first blow across the shoulders. A red streak appears on the white skin. Again the thongs are shaken out, again the hands rise, again the whips are brought down with full force, and the streak on the skin grows redder and broader. A turnkey gives out the number as each stroke falls; and the silence is broken only by his voice, by the descent of each successive blow, and by the cries or groans of the sufferer. But though there are instances in which the ruffian proves himself a coward, and yells with the very anticipation of pain before he has even been struck, there seems for the most part to be the same spirit in the flogging-room which the highwayman formerly displayed upon the gallows. The man who has been guilty of the most atrocious cruelty will do his best to conceal the smart which he is made to feel himself, and if any sound is heard from him at all, it proceeds from an involuntary action of his vocal organs which he strives his utmost to check. After twenty lashes he will retain a look of defiance, though almost fainting, and barely able to walk to his cell.

Anyone who has witnessed such a scene as this may be permitted to ask to what good end it is enacted; anyone who has not witnessed it can hardly be competent to judge of its good or ill effects. There is, no doubt, a dramatic fitness in punishing

the deliberate infliction of bodily pain by the deliberate infliction of bodily pain in return. And if the maxim 'an eye for an
eye and a tooth for a tooth' is a proper guide for lawgivers in a
Christian country in the nineteenth century, there remains nothing more to be said except that the 'cat' is, in many cases, too
merciful an instrument. If, however, the object of punishment
is not vengeance but the prevention of breaches of the law, it
seems useless, so far as example is concerned, to flog a prisoner
within the prison walls. The whole power of such a deterrent as
flogging (if it is to be regarded as a general deterrent), must lie
in the vividness with which it can be presented to the imagina-
tion of persons who have a tendency to commit, but who have
not yet committed, the offences for which flogging may be
legally inflicted. But the most ready manner of bringing it
home to the mind of the populace is by exhibiting it in public,
which, as has already been shown, has the very opposite effect
from that which is desired. The fact that the lash has been administered to a convict is now and again brought to the knowledge of the public by the press, and sometimes with the aid of
illustrations. But the impression made, so to speak, by such
exhibition at second-hand, cannot be so forcible as that made
by the old form of exhibition at first-hand; and in proportion as
it becomes effectual at all, it must be attended by the effects
which are produced by all brutal punishments inflicted *coram
populo.* L. O. Pike. *A History of Crime in England* . . . (1876), Vol
II, 575–7

---

30 John Wade   The Prison Hulks

John Wade (1788–1875), a journalist and historian, was
leader-writer on the *Spectator* from 1828 to 1858, and the
author of *The Extraordinary Black Book* (1820–3), a vitriolic
attack on what would now be called the Establishment. In
1829 he produced a more mildly written survey of the law-
enforcement system of London on the eve of Peel's reforms.
The passage that follows is a calm and dispassionate account
of the hulk system.

The convicts having accumulated greatly in the year 1776, and the intercourse with America being closed, it became necessary to resort to some other expedient; and, in the choice of difficulties, the system of the *hulks* was suggested and adopted, under the authority of the 16th of George the Third.

As is generally known, the hulks are large vessels without masts, which have been line-of-battle ships or frigates, and are moored near a dock-yard, or arsenal, so that the labour of the convicts may be applied to the public service. The present establishment consists of 10 vessels, on board of which have been usually confined, at one time, for some years past, between 3000 and 4000 convicts. The average number daily, during the year 1826, was 3609, and, in 1827, 4262. The principal stations are at Deptford, Woolwich, Chatham, Sheerness, and Portsmouth. One ship, the *Euryalus*, is appropriated exclusively for the reception of boys not exceeding 16 years of age, most of whom are taught trades—shoemaking, tailoring, bookbinding, &c. Very few of the adults work at trades, they are employed in everything the most laborious the Navy-Board and Ordnance Department can find them to do, in removing ballast out of and into ships, cleaning the ships out, taking up the mooring-chains, clearing the mud from the docks, and, since the disuse of horses, in removing and drawing all the timber.

It is only the convicts sentenced to short terms that are usually kept on board the hulks; those for life and fourteen years are sent to New South Wales; unless, under peculiar circumstances, the Secretary of State orders their detention in this country. On their arrival at the hulks, from the different gaols, they are immediately stripped and washed, clothed in coarse grey jackets and breeches, and two irons placed on one of the legs, to which degradation every one must submit, let his previous rank have been what it may. They are then sent out in gangs of a certain number to work on shore, guarded by soldiers. A strict account is kept of the labour performed by each gang, there being a scale by which it is calculated, and out of each shilling earned for the Government, by the convict, he is entitled to a penny, which is carried to his credit; but of this he receives only one-third part weekly, the remainder being left to accumulate until the expiration of the term which he is doomed to serve; thus it sometimes happens that a man who has been six or seven years on board the hulks, on his discharge is put in possession of £10 or £12, and is also supplied with an additional sum of money to defray his travelling-expenses home. The diet of each, for one week, is barley 1lb. 12oz., oatmeal 1lb. 5oz., bread 8lb. 12oz., beef 3lb. 8oz., cheese 12oz., salt 3½oz., small beer 7 pints. Those whose behaviour is exemplary are favoured by their term of punishment being shortened, or their irons lightened, or promotion to little offices, which relieves from severer labour. The number of convicts annually returned upon society from this source, by pardon or otherwise, amounts to about 600. . . . The hulks are not visited by the magistrates, and a large body of criminals are therefore placed exclusively under the jurisdiction of the Home Secretary of State; they are only visited occasionally by the superintendent appointed by him, and who resides in London, and reports twice-a-year, to the Secretary of State, upon the condition of the convicts.

The captain of each vessel has the privilege of recommending, as deserving of free pardons, a certain number of the prisoners (viz. two in 100) every three months. This extraordinary power has never been extended to the keeper of any gaol, nor should such a privilege be vested in any single officer. In the hulks it is customary to allow convicts to receive money from their friends, and to purchase therewith food of a better description than that afforded by the regulations. No such indulgence is permitted in a county gaol, except in particular instances, at the discretion of the magistrates. The convicts on board the hulks are allowed a portion of their earnings to be similarly expended.

The want of classification and of proper inspection are, however, the principal defects of the hulk system, if considered as a system, for the punishment and reformation of offenders.

Various efforts have been made to introduce better discipline and management, but, from the limited space and construction of ships, these advantages do not appear to be attainable. Without classification any place of confinement must necessarily be a school of vice, and prisoners discharged from the hulks are manifestly *hardened in depravity*. The fact is too notorious to require any statement of individual cases. J. Wade. *A Treatise on the Police and Crimes of the Metropolis . . .* (1829), 365–7

31 Transportation to Australia

Some of those confined in the hulks were ultimately sent to Australia, and the fate of those for whom transportation actually meant what it said was examined at frequent intervals—there were Select Committees on the topic in 1810–12, 1819, 1837–8, 1847, 1856 and 1861, and a Royal Commission in 1863. One reason for the frequency of inquiry was the difficulty, particularly acute in the earlier part of the century, at a time when the journey from England to Australia could take nearly six months, of knowing what was happening so far away. There was much conflicting evidence as to the fate of the convicts in Australia. Some wrote home to say that they were better off than ever before (31a) but the report of the Select Committee of 1837 emphasised the danger of relying on such letters, and the very wide range of possible fates, from very good to very bad, that could await a convict (31b).

(*a*)

Copy of a Letter from *William Vincent* to Mrs. *Vincent*, Pittdown, Fletching, Sussex.

Dear Mother, August 17, 1829.

I write these few lines, hoping to find you in good health, as it leaves me at present, and all my brothers and sisters, all friends and foes, which I am very glad to inform you that I am very happy, and I hope you are the same when you receive this letter. I am in a good place; I drive the governor's cart from

Parramatta to Sydney; and I hope you will let me know how you all be as soon as you can; and we had a very pleasant voyage, but it was very hot crossing the line of the sun; and the Bay of Biscay was very rough, and it is night there when it is day here; and I inform you that snakes is very bad in this country; we ofttimes see from 14 to 16 feet long. Parrots is as thick as crows in your country; Kangaroos too. But Henry Hart, I do not know where he is. Mutton is 4*d*. lb., beef 4*d*. And send word how Foster is, and Tema; and I thought oftentimes of David, because he never was well, and I shall be glad to hear of you all well, as I am at present; and when my time is out I shall come home, if God spares my life, and I hope to see you all well when I return. When this you see, remember me, and banish all trouble away from thee; which some people thought they had put me in great deal trouble, which they would, some of them, be glad to be as well as me; and I hope you are, mother, for I live at the governor's table, along with the other servants; and when you send me a letter, direct to New South Wales, Parramatta, Government Domain. So no more at present from your loving son,

William Vincent.

I forgot to tell you how far; it is 17,000 miles.

COPY of a LETTER from *Henry Tingley* to *Thomas Tingley*, Newick, near Uckfield, Sussex.

Dear Mother and Father, Ansley, 15 June 1835.

THIS comes with my kind love to you, hoping to find you in good health as, thank God, it leaves me at present very comfortable indeed. I have a place at a farm-house, and I have got a good master, which I am a great deal more comfortable than I expected. I works the same as I were at home; I have a plenty to eat and drink, thank God for it. I am allowed two ounces of tea, one pound of sugar, 12 pounds of meat, 10 pounds and a half of flour, two ounces of tobacco, the week; three pair of shoes, two suits of clothes, four shirts, a year; that is the allowance from Government. But we have as much to eat as we like, as some masters are a great deal better than others. All a man has got to mind is to keep a still tongue in his head, and do his master's duty, and then he is looked upon as if he were at home; but if he don't, he may as well be hung at once, for they would take you to the magistrates and get 100 of lashes, and then get sent to a place called Port Arthur to work in irons for two or three years, and then he is disliked by every one. I hope you will study these few lines which I have wrote to you, my dear mother and father, brothers and sisters and all my friends belonging to me in that country; this country is far before England in everything, both for work and money. Of a night, after I have done my work, I have a chance to make a few shillings; I can go out hunting or shooting of kangaroo, that is about the size of a sheep, or ducks or swans, tigers, tiger cats or native cats; there is nothing that will hurt a man but a snake, they are about five or six feet long, but they will get away if they can. I have dogs and gun of my own, thank God for it, to make me a few shillings, anything that I want; thank God, I am away from all beer-shops, there is ne'er a one within 20 miles of where I live. I have a fellow-prisoner living with me, which he is a shoemaker, and he is learning me to make shoes, which will be a great help to me; in about two years I shall be able to make a pair of shoes myself; then, thank God for it, I am doing a great deal better than ever I was at home, only for the wanting you with me, that is all my uncomfortableness is in being away from you. . . .

Henry Tingley.

PP, XIX (1837), 676–7

(b) Select Committee of 1837

Your Committee consider that in the preceding pages they have fully established the fact, that Transportation is not a simple punishment, but rather a series of punishments, embracing every degree of human suffering, from the lowest, consisting of a slight restraint upon the freedom of action, to the highest, consisting of long and tedious torture; and that the average amount of pain inflicted upon offenders in consequence of a

sentence of Transportation is very considerable. The most important question, however, as to the efficacy of Transportation
as a punishment, is not with regard to the actual amount of pain
inflicted, but the amount, which those who are likely to commit
crime, believe to be inflicted. It is proved, beyond a doubt, by
the testimony of every witness best acquainted with the actual
condition of convicts, and likewise by numerous facts stated in
the evidence, that most persons in this country, whether belonging to the criminal population, or connected with the administration of justice, are ignorant of the real amount of
suffering inflicted upon a transported felon, and underrate the
severity of the punishment of Transportation. Nor is this to be
wondered at, when it is considered, that the penal colonies are
16,000 miles distant, and that the ignorant mass of the criminal
population of this country are often misled by their evil passions
to underrate the consequences of their evil deeds. On their
arrival at the antipodes, they discover that they have been
grievously deceived by the accounts transmitted to them, and
that their condition is a far more painful one than they expected.
For those convicts who write to their friends an account of their
own fate, are generally persons who have been fortunate in the
lottery of punishment, and truly describe their lot in flattering
terms; those, on the other hand, who really experience the evils
of Transportation, and are haunted with "a continual sense of
degradation," are seldom inclined to narrate their sufferings
except when they have powerful friends from whom they may
expect assistance. Numerous instances, likewise, were mentioned of convicts, who, degraded and demoralized by their
punishment, have, from feelings of anger and revenge, indulged
in the malicious satisfaction of denying the efficacy of the law,
and of braving those who had brought them to condemnation,
by describing as pleasures the tortures they were enduring, by
affecting indifference for a punishment, which other criminals
were actually committing murder and seeking death in order to
avoid. Thus it is proved by the most irrefragable testimony,
that both those who are prosperous and those who are miserable,

the drawers of prizes and the drawers of blanks in this strange
lottery, influenced perhaps by that desire, common to human
nature, of having companions and partakers whether of misery
or of happiness, concur in tempting their friends in this country,
by the most alluring descriptions, to come out and join them;
thereby tending to diminish the little apprehension, if any,
which is entertained by the lower orders for the punishment of
Transportation. Both reason and experience, therefore, prove
that the utmost apprehension which the generality of offenders
feel for Transportation is little more than that they would
experience for simple exile, which, next to Transportation, is,
perhaps, the most unequal of punishments. . . .

The pain of exile depends upon the nature and strength of
the ties which connect an offender with his native country.
Exile is, therefore, a very severe punishment to persons who
have strong affections for their native land, for their kindred,
and for their acquaintances. Generally speaking, it is most
dreaded by those offenders against the laws of their country,
who may be termed accidental criminals; that is to say, by
persons who have not made a trade in crimes, but who have
been induced to commit crimes by the impulse of the moment,
or by some accidental combination of circumstances, or by
some all powerful temptation; and who may, in many cases, be
possessed of good moral feelings. On the other hand, exile is
least dreaded by the most numerous class of offenders, by those
who may be termed habitual criminals, and who compose what
is properly called the criminal population of this country,
namely, regular thieves, pickpockets, burglars, and all persons
who gain their livelihood by the repetition of offences, and who
consequently have lost all feelings of moral aversion to crime,
and can only be restrained by fear. The apprehension, which
this class of offenders feel for the punishment of exile, amounts
merely to an aversion to breaking off their criminal habits and
connexions in this country; on the other hand, to them the consequences of abstaining from a life of crime would be, that they
must equally separate themselves from their friends and asso-

ciates of the criminal class in this country, and lead a life of honest industry in a country where wages are low and the price of food is high; to such criminals this course of life must seem almost as disagreeable as, if not more disagreeable than, the chance of exile to Australia, where they understand that wages are high, and that their condition will be a comfortable one; that at all events they will obtain plenty of food and clothing, and that they will meet a number of ancient companions in crime, some of them in the most prosperous circumstances. Consequently, amongst such individuals, especially amongst London thieves and the like, the threat of expatriation produces little or no motive to induce them to abstain from criminal acts. The punishment of exile is, however, sometimes viewed with apprehension by offenders from the agricultural districts, who entertain a vague and ignorant horror of being removed from the land of their birth; this feeling is one which Your Committee can hardly think it advisable to encourage, nor can they deem it wise to stigmatize emigration by associating with it the idea of degradation and punishment, when they take into consideration the advantages which it holds out to the poorer orders of the community, to those who are most likely to be exposed to criminal temptations. Moreover, the great and yearly increasing emigration to all the British colonies, even to the penal ones, must soon, at all events, deprive exile to Australia of all its imaginary terrors.

Transportation, though chiefly dreaded as exile, undoubtedly is much more than exile; it is slavery as well; and the condition of the convict slave is frequently a very miserable one; but that condition is unknown, and cannot be made known; for the physical condition of a convict is generally better than that of an agricultural labourer; the former is in most cases better fed and better clothed than the latter; it is the restraint on freedom of action, the degradation of slavery, and the other moral evils, which chiefly constitute the pains of transportation, and of which no description can convey an adequate idea to that class in whom Transportation ought to inspire terror. . . . And what

description can a judge, or any other human being, give to an
offender of his future fate as a convict? Who can tell, what that
lot may be? A criminal sentenced to transportation may be sent
to New South Wales, or to Van Diemen's Land, or to Ber-
muda, or even to Norfolk Island; in each colony a different fate
would await him; his chance of enduring pain would be
different. In New South Wales, or even under the severer
system of Van Diemen's Land, he might be a domestic servant,
well fed, well clothed, and well treated by a kind and indulgent
master; he might be fortunate in obtaining a ticket of leave, or
a conditional pardon, and finish his career by accumulating
considerable wealth. Or he may be the wretched prædial slave
of some harsh master, compelled by the lash to work, until
driven to desperation, he takes to the bush, and is shot down
like a beast of prey; or for some small offence is sent to work in
chains, or to a penal settlement, where having suffered till he
can endure no longer, he commits murder in order that he may
die. Between these extremes of comfort and misery, there are
innumerable gradations of good and evil, in which the lot of a
convict may be cast. . . . Now, the mind of a person disposed to
commit a crime is precisely that of a gambler; he dwells with
satisfaction on every favourable chance, overlooks every adverse one, and believes that that event will happen, which is
most in accordance with his wishes. He hopes, that, if he commit a crime, he will escape detection; that, if detected, he will
escape conviction; that, if convicted, he will be pardoned or get
off with a few years in the hulks or Penitentiary; that, if transported, he will be sent to New South Wales; that, if sent to New
South Wales, he will be as well off, as are some of his acquaintances, and make a fortune. It is by diminishing the number of
chances in the criminal's favour, not by increasing the amount
of contingent evil; in other words, it is far more by the certainty,
than by the severity of punishment, that apprehension is produced, and thus Transportation sins against the first and
acknowledged principles of penal legislation. *PP*, XXII (1838),
19–21

32 Report of the Inspectors of Prisons

A major reform in prison administration, as in other fields during the period, was the introduction of inspectors who reported to Whitehall on the activities of local government. The Gaols Act of 1835 provided for the appointment of prison inspectors, and their reports to the Home Secretary were thereafter a primary source of information. They played a major part in the perennial nineteenth-century debate about methods of treatment in prison. In this extract from an early report, the prison inspectors call attention to the unsatisfactory features of imprisonment in gaols that still made very little provision for the classification of offenders of different types.

It is painful to reflect that the remedy provided by law for the correction of the offender, should only tend to render him more criminal. Of many children whom we have seen in prison, we hesitate not to affirm, that absolute impunity would have been far less mischievous than the effects of their confinement. It is notorious with what delight experienced thieves endeavour to corrupt those who are but just entering upon a criminal career. The detail of exploits, the most successful modes of committing depredations, the disposal of plunder, the narrative of escapes, the phraseology of thieves; these subjects are in the highest degree alluring to the young offender, and are eagerly discussed, in order to enliven and dispel the weariness of imprisonment. The first entrance of a boy into prison is almost invariably accompanied with feelings of alarm. No advantage, however, is taken of this favourable state of mind to inculcate good impressions. The boy is thrown among veterans in guilt, by whom his fears are derided, his rising penitence subdued, and his vicious propensities cherished and inflamed. Here he finds able and willing instructors in the perpetration of crime, and the foundation of every virtuous feeling becomes gradually destroyed. He enters the prison a child in years, and not unfrequently also in crime; but he leaves it with a knowledge in the ways of wickedness, which it is scarcely possible that he could acquire in any other place.

That this description is not overcharged, some idea may be formed, from the following sketch of the manner in which boys are confined in the prisons of the Metropolis.

Boys for trial by the Metropolitan Central Court are committed to Newgate. Others, who have been sentenced to transportation by that Court, are also frequently detained in this prison for some weeks after conviction. The elder of the juvenile prisoners, as well before as after conviction, are confined with the men, and are required to conform in all respects to the same regulations. No greater facilities can be conceived for the corruption of youth than are to be found in this prison. Boys committed for their first offence, and those whose guilt is doubtful, have no means of avoiding the society of hardened and atrocious offenders. There is no restraint on conversation; and the youth is consequently, soon after his admission, initiated by the most skilful instructors in all the arts of fraud and villainy. It has been seen that by the regulations of this gaol, any person assuming relationship with a prisoner may visit the Untried on three days in the week. Boys may consequently have intercourse with their former associates, and with girls of the most abandoned habits. The younger of the boys are generally collected in two apartments, with a view to keep them apart from the men; but they are not in fact (as we have shown) completely separated, as the room over one of these apartments is occupied by convicts who are employed as workmen in various parts of the prison. There is a common staircase and a common yard, and thus the workmen have access to the boys. Instruction is given in reading, during part of the day; but, except at these intervals, there is no kind of employment, and the nature of the confinement is calculated altogether to counteract any benefit which might, under other circumstances, be derived from the School. There is no separation by day or by night, and as the selection of the boys is guided by their age, all descriptions, whether tried or convicted, and every variety of offenders, are herded together. At the commencement of the last Session, twenty-four boys were in these apartments. Of this number, seven had been committed for robbing their masters, one for purloining from his father, and another from his aunt. One boy was charged with taking an article from a shop door, and another with stealing from a Yard. These lads were in close association, by day and night, with six pickpockets and three other boys, charged with stealing from a shop and dwelling-houses. Of the twenty-four, nine had been before (one of them four times) in confinement.

The prison in Giltspur Street is a Gaol, House of Correction, and Watch House. To this place are often committed boys before they have been taken to a Magistrate; others remanded for examination; others for trial; others convicted by sentences of the Central Court; others summarily convicted; and others apprehended at all hours of the day and night, for being disorderly in the streets. The prison is, in a great measure, an asylum for the houseless; and its wards and yards exhibit at all times a most disgusting accumulation of crime and destitution. The contracted space and crowded state of the Giltspur Street Compter render any approach to separation quite impracticable. The number of boys who are committed to this prison for being found abroad at night, or for other acts of vagrancy, is very considerable. As it is not possible to confine them apart from others, they are constantly placed in contact with notorious and hardened thieves. On a late visit we found several cases of this description: one, a sailor boy, who, having been ship-wrecked, had been committed to the prison as a place of refuge, until a vessel could be provided for him. This boy was in a ward with twelve men, some of whom had been remanded on charges of felony and embezzlement, and others convicted of various felonies and misdemeanors. And yet, objectionable as was this association for a boy simply destitute, and who had not been charged with any crime, there was no other part of the prison in which he could have been placed, with less danger to his morals. In the Vagrant Yard were several lads, objects of great destitution, in the closest intercourse with others who were notorious offenders. *PP*, V (1836), 88–9

33 Rev John Clay On the Separate System

The separate and the silent systems are explained in the first of the following extracts from the annual reports of the Rev John Clay (1796–1858), Chaplain of the House of Correction, Preston, from 1823 to the year of his death. Clay was an active writer on crime and criminals, and a forward-looking and perceptive reformer—his son and biographer could write of him, 'He was one of the first to teach the doctrine, common enough now, that the heartless selfishness of the upper classes, their disgraceful ignorance of, and indifference to, the brutal degradation in which they suffer the poor to lie, is the primary cause of almost all the crime in the country'. The emphasis on the power of religion in these passages, and the occasional feeling to which they give rise that the wool was at times drawn over Clay's eyes by the prisoners, do not enhance his reputation among modern readers; but the extracts convey well the attitudes of humane thinkers of the middle of the nineteenth century.

From Report for 1838

". . . The majority of the inspectors of prisons is in favour of the separate plan; by which is meant, the individual and entire seclusion of prisoners from each other, in cells of about 13 feet by 7, and 10 feet high, which are to be provided with every requisite for warmth, and ventilation, and cleanliness: the prisoners to be furnished with employment; to be visited daily by the principal officers, and to attend chapel on the Sabbath, under such regulations as shall ensure the integrity of the system. Many and powerful arguments are advanced in support of this plan, and there can be little doubt that it must have great advantages. Religious feelings, and the consequent probability of permanent reformation, are certain, in many cases, to be awakened in a solitude which is chiefly interrupted by the visits of the minister of religion. Contamination, if the system be perfectly administered, is impossible. While it has its consolations for the serious or devout, it has none whatever for the hardened; and is therefore adapted to reform the one, and deter the other. It may be said indeed to possess, as regards the characters of the confined, a *self-adjusting* principle. These are only a few, though probably the most prominent, of the reasons in favour of the plan of separation. The objections made to it must now be mentioned: they are, first, the very great expense which would be incurred by carrying out the system into full operation. 2d,—The tendency to insanity which it is said to produce in prisoners who undergo a long confinement. 3d,— The difficulty of providing suitable employment, especially such as would be available to the prisoner on his discharge; and, lastly, the fact, as stated in the report of the inspector of Scotland (a gentleman favourable, nevertheless, to the system), that at Glasgow, the only place in this country, I believe, where the plan has been fully tested, the recommittals are 50 per cent.

"The plan based upon the principle of *silence* is one which permits the employment of prisoners in sight of each other, but forbids the slightest degree of intercourse by words, signs, or looks; and provides for complete separation at night. This system is asserted 'to possess one superior quality among others —the placing men under trying circumstances where they are compelled to exercise, and may acquire, the valuable habit of self-control. At the same time social duties are kept in view; for it exacts respect to authority, order, cleanliness, decency at meals, and industry at labour.' The opponents of this plan maintain that the prisoner is kept in a constant and injurious state of excitement, by his inclination and efforts to evade the rule; and it is also alleged that there can be no security for the uniform rigour of its application.

"The plan of entire separation, if fully established, should guarantee its efficacy by the mere force of its leading principle. That of silence depends almost entirely upon the persons to whom the execution of it is committed."

From Report for 1840

"The effects, so far visible, of the plan of solitary confinement have been, to my mind, highly satisfactory; although *strict* non-intercourse, the principal essential to the full development of its benefits, is not yet enforced. But even under all the disadvantages incident to a first and imperfect trial of its power, the individual separation of prisoners has, I rejoice to say, operated in many cases most beneficially. . . . The plan at present adopted is incomplete, and may undergo some beneficial changes,— especially as the inspector of prisons for the district has not yet given the certificate which will authorise the cells to be used for any longer period of confinement than one month. As the routine now exists, the prisoner is enabled to take an hour's exercise daily, in silence, under the inspection of an officer; he attends prayers every morning, and also the services of the Sabbath; while such as are unable to read have the benefit of the schoolmaster's instruction. Three or four days elapse after they have received their sentence before I visit them; but when I do enter their cells with copies of the Holy Scriptures or other suitable books, it need hardly be said that my presence is evidently very acceptable to them; and I seldom take leave of the better disposed without an earnest request that I will repeat my visit at an early period. During the conversations which take place at these interviews, the prisoners, in many cases, have shown that softening of the heart which is evinced by tears. Among those who have attained mature age, and who have not been previously hardened by a long course of profligacy, this favourable and encouraging symptom is almost invariably met with; while it is seldom seen in the young criminals who are undergoing a second or third sentence. Their cases are the most hopeless. It is, alas! very melancholy to discover how easily, and rapidly, and permanently, corruption does its work upon the young! how soon feeling and principle, and the wholesome dread of disgrace, disappear, leaving behind no germ or remnant of good which might yet 'take root downward or bear fruit upward.' Although prisoners under fifteen are not more than one-fifth of the whole number [in solitary confinement, *i.e.* 101], they furnish almost the only instances of recommitment. Still, as regards boys whose irrepressible depravity does not necessitate their removal from the kingdom, this kind of discipline, especially when accompanied by whipping, offers the fairest prospect of advantage. . . . But it is for *men*, convicted of first offences, that this mode of correction holds out the greatest advantages. It is beyond my power adequately to describe the difference of manner and expression between those on the treadwheel and those in solitude. Indifference, levity, recklessness, characterize the demeanour of the majority of the former,—there are few traces of such qualities visible in the language and features of the latter; but on the other hand, a thoughtfulness—a saddening of the look and tone—the welcome evidences that the still small voices of memory and conscience have been heard; and that the solitary, debarred from all mischievous intercourse without, has been holding wholesome communion within. . . ."

From Report for 1847

". . . Adopting the main principle of individual separation, other and minor features of discipline are different in different prisons. In the Model Prison at Pentonville, where separation is enforced in its fullest integrity, a course of superior religious instruction is combined with instruction in a trade. To the attainment of these important objects twelve or eighteen months can be devoted, so that the prisoner on his removal as an *'exile'* is qualified, in every sense, to begin a 'new life.' In the prison at Reading, where *'encellulement'* is also most strict, the prisoners are employed *'in nothing but education.'* In the Glasgow Bridewell the paramount aim of the plan pursued, is the self-maintenance of the establishment. Here, in Preston, while the personal discipline is severe enough to deter such as give no hope of something better, our chief efforts are used to produce permanent amendment of character, by rousing into life and action the religious principle originally planted in the breast, and never altogether effaced. Order, cleanliness, and obedience, are enforced to a degree which must be most irksome to persons accustomed only to irregularity and dirt; two hours of active exercise, daily, preserves the bodily health, and keeps up elasticity of mind: instruction in reading, writing, arithmetic, &c., is given—and received—as a valuable privilege: work is supplied to all—except when compulsory idleness is inflicted for breach of prison rules,— and the value of regular occupation thereby taught;—and those who can exercise their trade in a cell, are permitted to do so,—a boon which is most highly valued. The prisoners assemble for daily and Sabbath worship, under circumstances which make them regard the Holy service as the greatest solace and advantage of their condition. . . .

From Report for 1850

"I am solicitous to have it understood that when I urgently recommend *separate* confinement, as the essential element of prison treatment, it is only because separation clears the way, more effectually than any other means hitherto devised, for the unimpeded operation of religious influences. Without these the cell would be not merely a useless, but a demoralizing cruelty. Remembering the mental and moral condition of the great bulk of our offenders, what would that condition become if delivered over entirely to the working, in solitude, of its own debasing tendencies? The inmate of the cell has, perhaps, lived—as too many do live—only in his animal instincts and appetites, and even in the depravation of *them*. Possessing no distinct apprehension of his eternal destiny, without the slightest knowledge of a Redeemer—of His power and love—born and bred in utter blindness to his spiritual state, *now* he feels his blindness, and, groping for light, can only obtain a glimpse of the flame which is 'never quenched.' Such a man as this—and I have seen too many of them—cannot *think*, he merely *remembers*—sometimes with horror, sometimes with wicked gratification. Should he strive to think, to comprehend his situation, the causes which

have led to it, the consequences yet to follow, the attempt is un-
availing: powers which, even if possessed, were never exercised,
can render no service *now*. Sooner or later a mental blank or a
mental anarchy succeeds, ending in sullen stupidity or wild
despair. That this is no overdrawn picture will be acknowledged by every one who knows the history of solitary confinement as first tried in the United States. But the separate cell,
which, in the absence of religion and her humanizing power,
was a curse, becomes, with her presence in it, a blessing. Her
minister enters it, assists the sufferer in giving discipline and
coherence to his feelings and conceptions, presents to his ex-
hausted mind food for hope, and to his conflicting passions the
prospect of peace. He unfolds the consoling truth that

> ——" 'All the souls that were, were forfeit once;
> And He who might the 'vantage best have ta'en
> Found out the Remedy.'

He persuades the downcast criminal that '*God is not willing that*
ANY *should perish.*' He persuades him that, even now, he is an
object of the Divine compassion, and that his repentance will
cause joy among the angels of Heaven. The value of the cell is
now manifest. Though it can never *originate* reformation, it is a
sure *promoter* of it." W. L. Clay. *The Prison Chaplain: A Memoir of
the Rev J. Clay, B.D.* . . . (Cambridge, 1861), 140–3, 278, 300

34 Rev John Field   Numbers and Masks
The problem of 'contamination', which the prison inspectors
had described and which the separate and silent systems
sought to overcome, was further combated by the means
described in the following extract—an interesting example of
the way in which humane motives could lead men into what
we now regard as inhumane and dehumanising conduct. The
Rev John Field was Chaplain of Reading Gaol from 1840 to
1858. The prison was known at the time as the 'Read, Read,
Reading Gaol', because prisoners had only a Bible for company.

There are two peculiarities in the prison dress which require a more particular description. There is attached to the left side of every prisoner's coat, a swivel, and when placed in his cell he is instructed that he is never to leave it again during the period of his imprisonment without affixing to this a brass circular plate, on which are inscribed a letter and a number corresponding with those of his cell. He is also directed that during attendance at Divine service, and when receiving instruction in class, this must be suspended on a hook above him. The name of the prisoner is of course often known to the officers who hold frequent communication with him, but it is never mentioned in the hearing of the other criminals. By his number he is constantly designated. The prudence, foresight, and humanity of such a regulation might be thought too apparent to require explanation; yet it has been the subject of mistake or misrepresentation. The only object aimed at, and the only end attainable by such means is to prevent either recognition by other prisoners; or if the inmates had been previously unknown to each other, then to prevent an acquaintance being formed, which could afford no possible advantage, but might, and probably would, be followed by injury both to society and to the criminal himself.

There would, however, be little security against such recognition, and its consequent evils, effected by the mere concealment of the name, if the features of the prisoner were exposed; a further precaution is therefore required.

In disguising even criminals, and although with a purpose so merciful and wise, it would have been improper to subject them to present suffering either of mind or body, and unjust to inflict any permanent injury. It was politic and kind to invent if possible some means which might not prove offensive; and this has been most charitably and effectually accomplished. The prisoner on leaving his cell, and when in sight of others, wears a cap with a peak, so constructed as to hide the greater part of his face, but with holes which allow him to see with as much ease as when without this covering. . . . That such a provision is desirable, surely none can doubt, and that it is necessary for the good of the individual, and for the welfare of society, must be almost equally evident. Yet the most strange ideas have been formed, and representations made of this merciful provision. J. Field. *Prison Discipline: And the Advantages of the Separate System* . . . 2nd ed, Vol I (1848), 194–6

35 Thomas Archer   Prison Occupations

Nineteenth-century prisoners spent much time picking oakum—pulling to pieces old and tarry ropes for use in caulking the planks of wooden ships. The trade had the merits that it was easily learned and easily controlled, and that there was a steady demand for its product. Another frequent form of prison labour was the treadmill. Both are described here by Thomas Archer, author of two books on criminal life.

A large square lobby, in appearance like a wheelwright's shed, in which coils of rope occupy some high shelves, and where men, standing at wooden blocks, are cutting old cable into chunks with small hatchets, leads to the series of rooms in which the prisoners are engaged in that most common employ-ment for vagrants or incorrigible paupers and convicted felons —picking oakum.

The hard pieces of junk are placed in a scale and weighed before being consigned to the basket in which they are con-veyed to the oakum rooms, the quantity which each prisoner has to pick daily, varying according to his sentence, that is to say, whether it be to hard labour or only to common imprison-ment; the former condemning him to pick from three to six pounds a day, in proportion to the hardness and tarriness of the junk, the latter to pick only two pounds a day. Notwithstanding that the carpenters', coopers', smiths', and other shops are busy, that the prison work in the way of plastering, painting, shoe-making, and tailoring, is done by convicts, and that the very tin porringers in which the food is dispensed are made by the prison tinsmiths, oakum picking is the busiest employment in the place, since the demand for oakum is insatiable. It is a trade soon learnt, and requires but little space for its execution. There are three oakum rooms, one for those imprisoned for misdemeanour and two in the felons' prison, and in all of these the men sit about two feet apart, on low forms, each picker with a heap of junk cut in pieces of a few inches long beside him, and with a small iron hook strapped just above his knee. As each length of rope is taken from the heap it is untwisted into separate strands, which are rolled backward and forward on the knee, or rubbed briskly under the iron hook, after which the fibre is easily picked into a fluffy ball, which goes to the heap of oakum on the right hand of the operator.

. . . the prisoners sit in these large rooms, twisting, rolling, rubbing, until their soft, thievish fingers grow red and sore, and afterwards hard by their contact with those stiff chunks of tarry hemp. . . . In the midst of these large rooms the warders on duty sit on elevated stools supporting frames which somewhat resemble portable reading-desks, and these officers watch keenly for any breach of discipline or an attempt at communication. . . .

The tread-mill, or, as it should be called, tread-wheel, . . . occupies one side of this room, . . . where some forty "hard-labour" felons are engaged in ascending a sort of revolving paddle-box, commanding no view whatever, and the top of which they never reach.

The tread-wheel alternates with oakum picking in the case of prisoners consigned to hard labour, and there are four or five wheels in the prison; the one which is now before me being the largest. The tread-wheel, which was first brought into use at Brixton prison in 1817, is said to have been the invention of Mr. Cubitt, the engineer of Lowestoft, who, on being adjured by one of the magistrates of the county jail at Bury, to invent some mode of employing the idle prisoners, was suddenly struck with the notion of an elongated wheel, which resulted in the invention of the machine that has been the terror of idle scoundrels ever since, and is generally known among them as "the mill."

F

The wheel, which is, in fact, a cylinder extending the whole length of the building, contains twenty-four steps, something like those used to mount a paddle-box; the circumference of this cylinder is sixteen feet, and the steps are eight inches apart, so that a revolution of the "wheel" includes twenty-four steps. At every thirtieth revolution, that is to say, every fifteen minutes, a bell connected with the machine, announces that the "spell" of work, which lasts a quarter of an hour, is finished, and on the days that a prisoner is set to work at the "mill," he completes fifteen of these spells, or nearly four hours of the hardest labour to which any human being need be subjected. There are three tiers or galleries in front of this wheel, where the prisoners can never mount the terrible steps which sink beneath the tread of each unhappy Sisyphus, as he holds with the ends of his fingers the ledge which extends at about the height of his shoulders. Each prisoner is divided from his neighbour by a woodwork screen, shaped like the end of a "box" in a coffee-room. . . . It is easy to see, too, that experience will enable the prisoner at the tread-wheel to avoid the labour to which the novice is subject by his endeavours to mount the steps, instead of allowing them to come down to the proper level, and sliding his foot easily upon each in succession. I notice, too, that some of the unfortunates seek to rest the ankle by a change of position and place first one and then the other foot sideways upon the narrow step. Whatever expedients they may adopt, however, there is no doubt that this at least is hard labour. If I ever had a doubt of it, that doubt is removed, as I see the men come down hot, panting, and bathed in perspiration, to sit on the benches at the bottom of the gallery; while others take their places in the vacant stalls to keep the relentless cylinder in motion. The amount of resistance of the wheel is regulated according to the number of men employed upon it, by a "governor" and a horizontal fan placed on a pedestal in the adjoining yard; but I am glad to learn that this exhausting labour is no longer useless, since it has been applied to the grinding of the prison flour, which is now pouring from the

hopper in a neighbouring apartment, fitted like a mill, while
the miller himself, with every appearance of that jollity pro-
verbial to his calling, is sitting amidst his sacks reading a news-
paper. T. Archer. *The Pauper, the Thief and the Convict* . . .
(1865), 157–9, 161–3

---

36 James Greenwood   In Prison—and On Release
James Greenwood, a journalist and novelist, won himself
renown by spending a night in a workhouse and describing
his experiences in the *Pall Mall Gazette* in 1866. Much of his
journalistic writing was reprinted in book form, like the two
passages quoted here. Both were based on contacts with
prisoners. The first is written by, or as if by, someone who has
served a sentence of three years' penal servitude, going first to
Newgate, then to Millbank, and finally to Pentonville. The
second is a thoughtful and sympathetic account of the difficulties facing prisoners on release—in essence unchanged
over the years.

(*a*)
Soon as we reached Pentonville we were again stripped and
bathed, a suit of clothes lying ready for each bather. The
clothes were as nearly as possible like those of Millbank, but the
cell in which I presently found myself was more cheerful looking
than the one at Millbank, and more resembled that at Newgate,
with the additional convenience of a drawer fixed under one of
the shelves. By-the-way, I should have mentioned that after
bathing, and before dressing, the doctor made his appearance
and thoroughly examined me, and asked me just the same sort
of questions as I have heard that they ask people who go to
insure their lives. Nor are they at Pentonville more careless
about your education than your bodily health. The very first
visitor that came to my cell was the schoolmaster, who sounded
me as to the extent of my scholastic knowledge, and shortly
afterwards supplied me with two books of arithmetic, a geo-
graphy, a dictionary, an atlas, and a slate and pencil; which,

with the Bible, and Prayer-book, and Hymn-book brought with me from Millbank, made quite a show, ranged on my shelf. Beside these books, if you behave as you ought, you are allowed to borrow one from the school library, the library books being of the "Leisure Hour" and "Sunday at Home" kind. I had but one half-day at school in a week, but there were some —the most ignorant—who had two half-days. The prison chapel is used as the school-room, and the same rule as regards keeping silence towards each other is observed as rigidly there as in every other part of the prison. There are two warders on duty in the school-room, perched in something like pulpits, so that they can see all about them. But they cannot stop talking entirely either in the school or in chapel; at the latter place especially it is indulged in. The prisoners sit in gangs all in a row of a dozen or so, every prisoner having a space of about six feet between himself and his neighbour, a warder being attached to each gang to see that order is kept. Some of the old hands, however, are too knowing for him. Long practice has taught them how to talk without moving their lips, and it is not uncommon to see the warder in command staring his hardest along the row and scrutinizing the face of every man with a most perplexed face of his own. He is certain that talking in an undertone is going on. He can hear the mysterious sounds, but every face is to the right and every eye devoutly fixed on the parson. . . .

The food at Pentonville is very fair both as to quantity and quality. You get beef and mutton on alternate days, with enough bread and vegetables; and cocoa for breakfast and gruel for supper. The labour is performed in the privacy of your own cell, and if you don't know a trade they teach you one. They taught me shoemaking. . . .

Nor is your work altogether unprofitable to you as regards wages. For the first six months—until, indeed, as I suppose, they think you know your trade—you get no remuneration at all: but after six months you get pay—sixpence a week if you are simply industrious, and eightpence if you are classed with the first grade, and known as very industrious. There is a third grade—the idle grade. Every day a mark is set against the names of the idle ones, and after these have been allowed a certain amount of rope, as the saying is, they are taken before the governor, who on a first charge simply warns them; if they continue idle, the effects of a week of bread and water is tried on them. There is another good thing, besides coming to be a wages man, that happens at the end of six months— for the first time since leaving Millbank he is allowed to see a visitor. . . .

You get a clean shirt and stockings and neckerchief once a week at Pentonville, and a clean flannel shirt and drawers once a fortnight. A bath once a fortnight. For exercise you are allowed to tramp round a circle made of paving stones in the yard. There are three circles, one within the other, with warders outside and within the circles, and you go round and round for an hour. At one time, in order to be sure that every man kept at a proper distance from his neighbour, there was a rope long enough and with knots in it at equal distance; while he was taking his walk, each convict held one of these knots in his hand, and it was the warder's duty to see that the rope through its whole extent was kept "taut." In wet weather you get no exercise in Pentonville, and sometimes when it sets in for a long spell of rain—the weather being always dull and heavy at such times—you have a rather miserable time of it. However, all get exercise when it is possible—even the refractory ones do who are condemned to the dark cells. There is a sort of round-house, divided into sections, with partitions too high to be overlooked, and up and down this "chicken-walk," as it is called, this class of prisoner tramps his allotted time in company of two warders. J. Greenwood. *The Wilds of London* (1876), 41–3

(*b*)

He comes out of prison, determined to reform. But where is he to go? What is he to do? How is he to live? Whatever may have been done for him in prison, is of little or no avail, if as soon as he leaves the gaol he must go into the world branded with crime, unprotected and unhelped. The discharged prisoner must be friendly with some one, and he must live. His criminal friends will entertain him on the understood condition that they are repaid from the booty of his next depredation. Thus the first food he eats, and the first friendly chat he has, becomes the half necessitating initiative of future crime. Frequently the newly discharged prisoner passes through a round of riot and drunkenness immediately on his release from a long incarceration, as any other man would do in similar circumstances, and who has no fixed principles to sustain him. And so by reason of the rebound of newly acquired liberty, and the influence of the old set, the man is again demoralized. The discharged prisoner leaves gaol with good resolves, but the moment he enters the world, there rises before him the dark and spectral danger of being hunted down by the police, and being recognised and insulted, of being shunned and despised by his fellow workmen, of being everywhere contemned and forsaken.

There can be no doubt that to this utter want of friends of the right sort at the moment of leaving prison, may be attributed a very large percentage of the persistence in a career of crime by those who have once made a false step. In this respect we treat our criminals of comparatively a mild character with greater harshness and severity than those whose repeated offences have led to their receiving the severest sentences of the law. The convict who is discharged after serving a term of five years at Portland, receives ere he quits the gates of Millbank prison a money gratuity, varying in amount according to the character that was returned with him from the convict establishment. Nor do the chances that are afforded him of quitting his old course of life and becoming an honest man end here. There is the Prisoner's Aid Society, where he may obtain a little more money and a suit of working clothes, and if he really shows an inclination to reform, he may be even recommended to a situation. But for the poor wretch who has given society much less offence, who has become a petty thief, probably not from

choice, but from hard necessity, and who bitterly repents of his
offences, there is no one to take him by the hand and give or
lend him so much as an honest half-crown to make a fair start
with. It may be said that the convict is most in want of help
because he *is* a convict, because he is a man with whom robberies and violence have become so familiar, that it is needful
to provide him with some substantial encouragement lest he
slide back into the old groove. Further, because he is a man so
plainly branded that the most inexperienced policeman may
know at a glance what he is; whereas, the man who has been
but once convicted may, if he have the inclination, push his way
amongst honest men, and not one of them be the wiser as to the
slip he has made. And that would be all very well if he were
assisted in rejoining the ranks of honest bread-winners, but
what is his plight when the prison door shuts behind him? It
was his poverty that urged him to commit the theft that consigned him to gaol, and now he is turned out of it poorer than
ever, crushed and spirit-broken, and with all his manliness
withered within him. He feels ashamed and disgraced, and for
the first few hours of his liberty he would willingly shrink back
for hiding, even to his prison, because, as he thinks, people look
at him so. A little timely help would save him, but nothing is so
likely as desperate "don't care" to spring out of this consciousness of guilt, and the suspicion of being shunned and avoided;
and the army of twenty thousand gains another recruit.

This undoubtedly is frequently the case with the criminal
guilty of but a "first offence." Be he man or lad, however, he
will be subject to no such painful embarrassment on his leaving
prison after a second or third conviction. By that time he will
have made friends. He will have found a companion or two to
"work with," and they will keep careful reckoning of the date
of his incarceration as well as of the duration of his term of
durance. Make no doubt that they will be on the spot to rejoice
with him on his release. They know the exact hour when the
prison gate will open and he will come forth, and there they are
ready to shake hands with him. Ready to "stand treat." Ready

to provide him with that pipe of tobacco for which he has experienced such frequent longing, and to set before him the foaming pot of beer. "Come along, old pal!" say they, "we thought that you'd be glad of a drink and a bit of bacca, and we've got a jolly lot of beef over some baked taters at home!"

What becomes of all his good resolutions—of the chaplain's wholesome counsel now! J. Greenwood. *The Seven Curses of London* (?1869), 98–101

37 Gladstone Committee   Report

In 1894 growing discontent with the administration of the prisons, all now under the control of the Prison Commission and its Chairman Sir Edmund Du Cane, led to the appointment of a Departmental Committee on Prisons. The report of the Committee was a condemnation of the approach to prisoners then employed, and it laid down the lines that prison administration in this country has been following ever since. The Chairman of the Committee, the man who gave it his name, was Herbert J. Gladstone (1854–1930), youngest son of William Ewart Gladstone, and at the time Parliamentary Under-Secretary of State at the Home Office. He was chief whip of the Liberal Party 1899–1905, Home Secretary 1905–9, and Governor-General of South Africa 1910–14. He received a viscountcy in 1909.

5. . . . We could not but be cognisant of the circumstances under which the inquiry was instituted. In magazines and in the newspapers, a sweeping indictment had been laid against the whole of the prison administration. In brief, not only were the principles of prison treatment as prescribed by the Prison Acts criticised, but the prison authority itself, and the constitution of that authority, were held to be responsible for many grave evils which were alleged to exist. . . .

17. If the condition and treatment of prisoners at the present time are compared with what they were 60, 40, or even 20 years

ago, the responsible authorities can justly claim credit for great
and progressive improvement. The bad prisons have disappeared. In the full consciousness of these improvements, it
was not unreasonable that there should have been a somewhat
rigid adherence to the lines of the Prison Acts, and great faith
induced in the principles which they laid down. . . .

We do not consider, therefore, that there is reason for general
condemnation of a system which resulted originally from careful inquiry and much deliberation; and which was specially and
successfully designed to put an end to many glaring and patent
evils. . . . Nevertheless, we feel that the time has come when the
main principles and methods adopted by the Prison Acts
should be seriously tested by the light of acquired experience
and recent scientific research. . . .

23. . . . The great and, as we consider, proved danger of this
highly centralised system has been, and is one in which attention has been given to organisation, finance, order, health of the
prisoners, and prison statistics; the prisoners have been treated
too much as a hopeless or unworthy element of the community,
and the moral as well as the legal responsibility of the prison
authorities has been held to cease when they pass outside the
prison gates. The satisfactory sanitary conditions, the unbroken
orderliness of prison life, economy and high organisation, are
held, and justly held, to prove good administration. But the
moral condition in which a large number of prisoners leave the
prison, and the serious number of re-commitals have led us to
think that there is ample cause for a searching enquiry into the
main features of prison life. From the evidence submitted to us
it appears that as a criminal passes into the habitual class,
prison life, subject to the sentences now given, loses its terrors
as familiarity with it increases. . . .

25. . . . We think that the system should be made more
elastic, more capable of being adopted [sic—presumably
'adapted' was intended] to the special cases of individual
prisoners; that prison discipline and treatment should be more
effectually designed to maintain, stimulate or awaken the

F*

higher susceptibilities of prisoners, to develop their moral instincts, to train them in orderly and industrious habits, and
whenever possible to turn them out of prison better men and
women, both physically and morally, than when they came in.
Crime, its causes and treatment, has been the subject of much
profound and scientific enquiry . . . but . . . it would be a loss of
time to search for a perfect system in learned but conflicting
theories, when so much can be done by the recognition of the
plain fact that the great majority of prisoners are ordinary men
and women amenable, more or less, to all those influences
which affect persons outside. *PP*, LVI (1895), 5, 9, 11–12

38 The Work of M. D. Hill

One of those active in the campaign for a reform of the
treatment of juveniles was Matthew Davenport Hill (1792–
1872), a brother of Sir Rowland Hill. A lawyer of radical
sympathies, M. D. Hill was Recorder of Birmingham from
1839 to 1866, and in this capacity did much to promote the
reform of the criminal law. He was an active associate of
Mary Carpenter (see extract 11) in the promotion of reformatory schools, industrial schools and ragged schools. As this
extract explains, he was also a pioneer of the informal use of
probation, anticipating a method of treatment not given
legislative sanction until 1907 (by the Probation of Offenders
Act, 7 Ed VII, c 17).

For a period of seven years, beginning early in the year 1841,
he had thus acted with regard to juvenile offenders:—that when
there was ground for believing that the individual was not
wholly corrupt—when there was reasonable hope of reformation—and when there could be found persons to act as guardians
kind enough to take charge of the young convict (which at first
sight would appear to present a great difficulty, but which in
practice furnished little impediment to the plan), he had felt
himself justified in at once handing over the young offender to
their care, in the belief that there would be better hope of

amendment under such guardians than in the gaol of the county. And he was happy to say that the intelligent officer at the head of the police, informed him that a much greater number so disposed of were withdrawn from evil courses than of those who, having no such advantages, had been consigned to prison.

We take as much care as we can not to be imposed upon, either by too sanguine a hope of amendment, or from imperfect information as to the results actually obtained. At unexpected periods a confidential officer visits the guardian, makes inquiries, and registers the facts of which he is thus informed, in an account which has been regularly kept from the beginning. The results he would now submit to them. The number of young offenders so disposed of was 166; of these the conduct of 71 was good. Of the greater number of that 71 the good conduct had been of such long standing that he was warranted in assuming their reformation to be complete and assured. The conduct of 40 was doubtful. That was said partly because it had not been quite consistent, and partly because some of the lads had passed out of sight, and therefore could not be spoken of with certainty. Of 53 the conduct had been bad, and two were dead. He might observe that he had felt it his bounden duty to take care, when a youth so privileged had returned to his evil ways, and was again convicted before him, that his punishment should be such as to show that it was from no weakness, from no mistaken indulgence, from no want of resolution on the part of the Court to perform its duty, that a course of mildness had been pursued, but that such a chance had been offered because it had been found by experience not only merciful towards the individual, but profitable to the community. In those instances, therefore, in which the plan had failed, the safety of the public demanded a severe penalty. Nor was it less demanded for the permanent interests of the prisoner himself, because assuredly there was no indulgence more fatal to him who received it than a series of light punishments, which familiarized his mind to degradation, and left him in a path which would lead him, step by step, to the gravest crimes, and consequently to the heaviest inflictions known to the law.

The kindness of the Directors of one of the most valuable institutions in the county of Warwick—he meant the asylum at Stretton-upon-Dunsmoor—had enabled him to send there certain of the boys whose cases were more peculiarly deserving of benevolent care. . . . The gentlemen of the jury were aware that the asylum is not a prison, and that there are no physical means whereby the boys might be restrained from leaving it. As a matter of course, therefore, it followed that the means employed could only operate upon the mind and the heart, a circumstance which, although at first it might create its difficulties, was probably no slight cause of ultimate success.

From the year of foundation, up to 1827, the proportion of reformed was only 48 per cent; that is to say, when 100 boys were received, 48 were reformed, and 52 were cases of failure. But in 1843 the improvement was such that the reformed amounted to 56 per cent. In 1844 they reached 58; in 1846, 60 per cent.; and in 1847 the reformed had reached the proportion of 65 per cent. He was sure the Grand Jury would agree with him that this was a very encouraging state of affairs. M. D. Hill. *Suggestions for the Repression of Crime, Contained in Charges Delivered to Grand Juries of Birmingham* . . . (1857), 117–19

39 Reformatory Schools and Industrial Schools

The reformatory and industrial schools were regarded as being largely responsible for the drop in juvenile crime in the latter part of the nineteenth century, and these two extracts are typical of the tributes paid to them. The first comes from Henry Rogers, assistant inspector of reformatory and industrial schools, and the second from Mrs Helen Bosanquet (1860–1925), who was, like her husband Bernard, active in the Charity Organisation Society and was a member of the Royal Commission on the Poor Laws of 1905.

(*a*) *Evidence of Mr Henry Rogers, Assistant Inspector of Reformatories and Industrial Schools, to Departmental Committee on Prisons, 1894*

Question 2395. . . . The boys are not so criminal or so difficult to deal with as they used to be.

Q. 2396. Do you think the boys are less criminal now?—Certainly they are.

Q. 2397. Is that due to the gangs being broken up?—Yes, we do not have the same education in crime that we had. It is useless to attempt now to educate juveniles for a criminal career.

Q. 2398. You go back 40 years to the origin of reformatories?—I do.

Q. 2399. And you are aware that in those days there used to be regular training gangs of boys?—I am quite aware of it.

Q. 2400. And that in a very few years they entirely disappeared?—We have entirely broken up the gangs by the reformatories. The trainers say, "Oh, it is no use training boys now the gangs get broken up;" and they say, "What is the good of our training boys that will be sent to a reformatory; we have to begin over again; it is of no use." It is within my experience that there was not a railway station in London where trained juvenile thieves did not attend when the ladies came up with their pockets full of money and there were three or four of these trained boys always there. The lads have related to me their experience over and over again, and they said: "We have only just to dig our two fingers into a lady's pocket and out used to come five, six, or seven sovereigns." But we hear little of that kind now; we have broken up that system entirely. You can see even from the experience of everyday life that the newspapers do not report cases of pickpockets now; a few years ago there was nothing heard of in the police courts but "pocket dipping", as they called it, with two fingers. *PP*, LVI (1895), 134

(b) Helen Bosanquet

To a very large extent we have in London succeeded in putting a stop to the wholesale manufacture of pauperism and crime which had been going on. Perhaps the most important step towards its suppression was the Industrial Schools Act of 1866. By this Act magistrates were empowered to send to Industrial Schools all children (1) begging or receiving alms, (2) found wandering and not having any home or settled place of abode, or visible means of subsistence; (3) found destitute, either being an orphan, or having a surviving parent undergoing penal servitude; (4) frequenting the company of reputed thieves. Also all children under twelve where the child is charged with an offence punishable by imprisonment, but has not been convicted of felony; and all children under fourteen where the parent or step-parent represents that he is unable to control the child, and that he desires that the child be sent to an Industrial School.

Here, then, is an effective means, if wisely applied, for checking the children at the very beginning of their downward course; that they are not prevented from entering upon that course may be seen from the fact that in 1894 no less than 2,460 children were dealt with by the London School Board as coming within the provisions of this and similar Acts. It is interesting as showing the need for unremitting care, to note the classification of these little outcasts: 298 were described as begging; 435 as wandering or not under proper guardianship; 51 associating with reputed thieves; 62 as found in houses of ill-fame, &c.; 513 as stealing or any offence punishable by imprisonment; 153 as beyond parental control; 15 non-attendance, &c.; and not charged 78. The remaining 855 were merely "truants." H. Bosanquet. *Rich and Poor* (1898), 52–3

---

40 R. F. Quinton   Borstal

If the reformatory and industrial schools movement represented a success story in the treatment of juvenile offenders, much the same can be said, so far as the period before the First World War is concerned, of the Borstal system. The impact of this new method of treatment is described here by R. F. Quinton (1849–1934), who was a medical officer at a number of prisons before ending his career as Governor and Medical Officer of Holloway Prison.

The Prevention of Crimes Act, Part I, which deals with the reformation of young offenders between sixteen and twenty-one years of age . . . is of great importance. It is, in reality, based on the experimental treatment which the Prison Commissioners have been applying to youths of this age for several years past, and generally known as the Borstal System, and which has been attended with such striking success. It is based on the principles of strict discipline, tempered with several valuable rewards and privileges for good conduct and industry. The youth is made to work at some skilled trade in which he can take an interest, he goes through a regular daily course of physical drill, and, on the moral and intellectual side, his general education is specially forwarded, while he is encouraged to read literature that is improving as well as instructive, and he hears lectures on subjects that are likely to attract and interest him. The results of the scheme, so far, have been of a most encouraging nature. The material to be experimented on looked far from promising at first sight. Most of these young offenders had already apprenticed themselves to crime, and were on the high road to lives of professional criminality, having many previous convictions against their names for acts of larceny, hooliganism, and other kinds of lawlessness. They already bore the prison stamp, and—a worse feature still—gloried in it as a distinctive mark of heroism.

Medical examination showed that they were physically much below the proper standard of their age and class, while many were afflicted with disease, deformity, or disablement of some kind. It was soon found, however, that with proper training and physical drill the slouching and undersized loafers gained rapidly in height, weight, and chest measurement, and general muscular development, so as to acquire a smart, well-set-up appearance, which frequently heralded the dawning of self-respect. . . . Simultaneously, strong efforts were made to improve their general intelligence, and to add to their mental and moral equipment, and lastly, they were equipped with sufficient skill in some form of industry to enable them to make a fresh start in decent life.

Further, an After-Care Association was formed of benevolent people who took an interest in the rescue of young offenders, and these voluntary workers have contributed largely to the success of the scheme by giving freely time, money, and personal energy, by finding work for them on discharge from prison, and by keeping a kindly and watchful eye on their progress afterwards.

A modification of the system was also devised for those whose short sentences excluded them from the full benefits of the scheme, for which a period of at least twelve months was necessary.

The practical results are that from 60 to 70 per cent. of those who were dealt with under the full scheme are known to be at work and doing well, while 58 per cent. of those under the modified benefits are also known to be doing well, and 11 per cent. only have been reconvicted. R. F. Quinton. *Crime and Criminals 1876–1910* (1910), 121–4

Suggestions for Further Reading

A bibliography on this subject must start with L. Radzinowicz, *A History of English Criminal Law and its Administration from 1750*. Volume I, 'The Movement for Reform', discusses law reform and the repeal of capital punishment at the end of the eighteenth and the beginning of the nineteenth centuries; Volumes II, 'The Enforcement of the Law', and III, 'The Reform of the Police', present the background to Peel's reform of the policing of London in 1829; IV, 'Grappling for Control', carries the themes of all three earlier volumes through to the 1860s. The same author's *Ideology and Crime* contains a brief survey of the historical development of crime and of society's reaction.

For my own *Crime and Industrial Society in the Nineteenth Century* (retitled *Urban Crime in Victorian England* in its American paperback edition) I can claim at least that it is the only attempt to study its subject from the point of view of the social historian. Other books that have covered some of the same ground in a less academic vein are C. Hibbert, *The Roots of Evil*, and K. Chesney, *The Victorian Underworld*. A persuasive study of criminal conduct over several centuries is Mary McIntosh, 'Changes in the Organization of Thieving', in S. Cohen (ed), *Images of Deviance*. My article 'The Crime Industry', *British Journal of Criminology*, VI (1968) is an attempt to study criminal behaviour as an economist might study any other activity carried on for gain. L. Chevalier, *Classes laborieuses et classes dangereuses à Paris pendant la première moitié du 19ème siècle* provides the opportunity to compare nineteenth-century London with nineteenth-century Paris. The criminal statistics of the century are discussed in the forthcoming collective work *The Study of Nineteenth-Century Society*, edited by E. A. Wrigley.

The thoughts of the nineteenth-century writers on crime can be studied in H. Mannheim, *Pioneers in Criminology*; this should be supplemented by G. D. Robin, 'Pioneers in Criminology: William Douglas Morrison', *Journal of Criminal Law, Criminology and Police Science*, LV (1964), and P. Collins, *Dickens and Crime*. But many of the works of the people themselves are now being reprinted and will amply repay study. Special mention should perhaps be made of M. D. Hill and Mary Carpenter, and of the *First Report* of the Royal Commission on a Constabulary Force of 1839 (see the earlier extracts from these). Henry Mayhew's *London Labour and the London Poor* has been much quarried for material about criminals, but the fourth and most relevant volume is for the most part not by Mayhew but by lesser men, not above quoting without acknowledgement from the 1839 *Report* as well as from Mayhew's *Morning Chronicle* articles of 1849–50.

The student of police history should turn first to T. A. Critchley, *A History of Police in England and Wales 900–1966*. C. Reith is an indefatigable but rather naive student of police history—see his *The Police Idea, British Police and the Democratic Ideal* and *A New Study of Police History*. W. L. Melville Lee's *A History of Police in England* of 1901 is still worthy of study. Important articles are J. M. Hart, 'Reform of the Borough Police, 1835–56', *English Historical Review*, LXX (1955), 'The County and Borough Police Act, 1856', *Journal of Public Administration*, XXXIV (1956), and H. Parris, 'The Home Office and the Provincial Police in England and Wales, 1856–1870', *Public Law* (1961). A. Silver's 'The Demand for Order in Civil Society: A Review of Some Themes in the History of Urban Crime, Police, and Riot', in D. J. Bordua (ed), *The Police: Six Sociological Essays*, puts forward some interesting ideas which deserve further examination. I have offered a reappraisal of the value of the pre-Peel policing system in my introduction to the Patterson Smith reprint of John Wade's *A Treatise on the Crimes and Police of the Metropolis* of 1829, and in an article to appear in the *Journal of Contemporary History* in 1972.

A full study of Britain's prison system in the nineteenth century remains to be written, but the best introduction is R. S. E. Hinde, *The British Penal System, 1773–1950*. On transportation we are better served, with A. G. L. Shaw, *Convicts and the Colonies*, providing the general survey, W. D. Forsyth, *Governor Arthur's Convict System, Van Diemen's Land, 1824–36*, giving closer attention to an important aspect, and C. Bateson, *The Convict Ships*, providing the definitive study of its topic. L. L. Robson in *The Convict Settlers of Australia* reports on an analysis of a sample of transportees, and A. Hasluck, *Unwilling Emigrants—A Study of the Convict Period in Western Australia*, though a slighter work, offers a convincing picture of conditions.

Acknowledgements

The author would like to thank the following for permission to reproduce extracts from the works listed below: The Library of University College London (The Chadwick Papers); The NSPCC and Westminster Hospital (*A Child of the Jago* by Arthur Morrison); Stanley Paul & Company Limited (*White Slave Market* by O. C. Malvery); Macmillan & Company Limited, London and Basingstoke (*Rich and Poor* by B. Bosanquet); Longman Group Limited (*Crime and Criminals 1876–1910* by R. F. Quinton).

Index